實用烘焙

INTERNATIONAL BAKING DELIGHTS

作　　　者	林麗華
翻 譯 顧 問	葛潔輝
出　版　者	純青出版社有限公司
	台北市松江路125號4樓
	郵政劃撥12106299
	電話：(02)2508-4331・2507-4902
	網址：www.weichuan.org.tw
	E-Mail：We122179@ms13.hinet.net
著作財產權人	財團法人味全文化教育基金會
版 權 所 有	局版台業字第3884號
	中華民國85年5月初版發行
	中華民國88年9月二版發行
印　　　刷	合同美術印刷廠股份有限公司
定　　　價	新台幣參佰元整
Author	Lee Hwa Lin
Translation Consultant	Connie Wolhardt
Publisher	Chin Chin Publishing Co., Ltd.
	4th fl., 125, Sung Chiang Rd.,
	Taipei, Taiwan, R.O.C.
	Tel:(02)2508-4331・2507-4902
Distributor	Wei-Chuan Publishing
	1455 Monterey Pass Rd., #110
	Monterey Park, CA91754, U.S.A.
	Tel :(323)2613880・2613878
	Fax:(323)2613299
Printer	Ho Tong Art Printing Factory Co., Ltd.
	Printed in Taiwan, R.O.C.
Copyright Holder	Copyright © 1996
	By Wei-Chuan Cultural-Educational Foundation
	First Printing, May, 1996
	Second Printing, Sept., 1999
	ISBN 0-941676-68-4

序

　　每次經過西點麵包店，遠遠的就會被一股香噴噴的烘焙香味吸引住。尤其是在麵包將要出爐時，聞到香味都會令人情不自禁的跨入店裡，買些點心以解口饞。

　　很多人都誤認，在家裡自己做麵包是一件很困難的事。其實，如果有好的方法，用對的食譜，它跟做菜一樣簡單，而且做出來的點心不但會比店裡買的好吃，同樣也會對於添加物的問題較放心。尤其現在是個電器化的時代，幾乎每一個家庭都有烤箱的設備，烤箱的使用也越來越方便，因此要在短時間內烘焙出香噴噴的點心並不困難。

　　這本實用烘焙是味全家政班的老師們一年多來收集世界各國烘焙資料，再經過無數次的試作，才將最好的成果集結成書。本書共有七十七道食譜，分成麵包、派、蛋糕、甜甜圈、餅乾等類，它不但是國際性的食譜，也包含了台灣國家丙級烘焙考試的考題。

　　本書內容深入淺出，並且有很多小圖片可供使用者參考，是一本值得全家一起動手做的烘焙食譜。

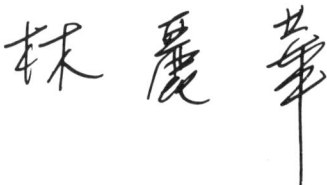

Forward

Everybody knows how wonderful the aromas are that surround a bakery ! The delightful scents tantalize the taste buds and melt away any resistance to the temptation to satisfy one's palate.

This "International Baking Delights" cookbook offers the reader the opportunity to create these delectable aromas, and of course the bakery treats, by just following any of the 77 simplified, thoroughly tested recipes. The recipes have been selected by instruction at the Wei-Chuan Cooking School from international favorites and designed to make the experience pleasurable, with each ingredient precisely measured to furnish the maximum taste enjoyment.

"International Baking Delights"cookbook makes home baking a simple matter, while earning compliments for the cook!

Lee Hwa Lin

目錄 Contents

餅乾類 . Cookies

奶油小西餅	Butter Fingers	10
花生醬小餅	Peanut Butter Cookies	10
奶油椰子小西餅	Coconut Butter Cookies	11
脆皮花生小西餅	Peanut Macaroons	11
巧克力小餅	Chocolate Cookies	12
葡萄乾燕麥紅糖小西餅	Oatmeal-Raisin Cookies	13
擠花小西餅	Piped Cookies	14
蛋黃小西餅	Cookie Sandwiches	15
冰箱小西餅	Refrigerator Cookies	16
巧克力白帽小西餅	Snow-Capped Cook Sandwiches	17
營養餅乾	Nutritious Biscuits	18
葡萄酥	Oblong Raisin Bars	19
杏仁酥條	Almond Bars	20
起司酥條	Cheese-filled Rolls	21
蝴蝶酥	Butterfly Pastries	22

甜甜圈類 . Doughnuts

空心泡芙	Basic Puffs	23
鮮蝦泡芙	Prawn Salad Puffs	23
火腿沙拉泡芙	Ham Salad Puffs	24
蒸烤雞蛋牛奶布丁	Caramel Pudding	24
咖啡愛克力	Coffee Eclairs	25
奶油泡芙	Cream Filled Puffs	26
酵母甜甜圈	Raised Doughnuts	27
馬鈴薯甜甜圈	Potato Doughnuts	28
豆沙甜甜圈	Bean Paste Filled Doughnuts	29
蛋糕甜甜圈	Cake Doughnuts	30
桔子麻花甜甜圈	Orange Twisters	31
三味甜甜圈	Doughnuts with Savory Fillings	32
三角鬆餅	Filled Pastry Deltas	34
鳳梨酥	Chinese Pineapple Cakes	35
菊花酥	Chrysanthemum Pastries	36
核桃酥	Walnut Cookies	37

派‧塔類 . Pies.Tarts

派皮製作	Basic Pie Shell	38
波士頓派	Boston Pie	39
轉化糖漿	Invert Syrup	40
鹼水	Lye	40
塔皮製作	Basic Tart Shell Dough	41
蛋塔	Custard Tarts	41
加拿許塔	Canache Pie	42
黑櫻桃杏仁塔	Black Cherry Tarts	42
杏仁塔	Almond Tarts	43
核桃塔	Walnut Tarts	44
草莓戚風派	Strawberry Chiffon Pie	45
巧克力戚風派	Chocolate Chiffon Pie	46
鮮肉小派餃	Petite Pork Pies	47
廣式月餅	Cantonese Moon Cakes	48
蛋黃酥	Oriental Surprises	49

蛋糕類 . Cakes

蛋白打發程度	Guide to whisk egg whites	50
小蛋糕	Cup Cakes	51
海綿蛋糕	Sponge Cake	51
香草天使蛋糕	Vanilla Angel Cake	52
奶油蛋糕	Butter Cake	52
乳酪蛋糕	Processed Cheddar Cheese Cake	53
菠蘿蛋糕	Pineapple Cake	54
美式輕鬆草莓蛋糕	American Strawberry Cake	55
檸檬蛋糕	Lemon Chocolate Cakes	56
臉譜蛋糕	Small Decorative Cakes	57
千層蛋糕	Layered Cake	58
大理石蛋糕	Marble Cake	59
巧克力戚風蛋糕	Chocolate Chiffon Cake	60
香草戚風蛋糕	Vanilla Chiffon Cake	61
迷你卡通蛋糕	Mini Cartoon Cakes	62
巴巴樂蛋糕	Bavarian Cream with Fruits	63
葡萄戚風捲	Raisin Swiss Roll	64

麵包類 . Breads

軟式甜麵糰	Basic Sweet Roll Dough	65
熱狗捲	Hot Dogs in Buns	66
蘋果麵包捲	Apple Rolls	67
椰子玉米麵包	Corn - Coconut Buns	68
紅豆麵包	Rolls with Red Bean Filling	69
乳酪麵包	Ham - Cheese Buns	70
玉米火腿麵包	Corn - Ham Buns	71
地瓜麵包	Rolls with Yam Filling	72
香脆馬鈴薯麵包	Potato and Cheese Rolls	73
布丁餡甜麵包	Custard Filled Rolls	74
橄欖形餐包	Oblong Dinner Rolls	75
蘋果沙拉麵包	Buns with Apple Salad Filling	77
墨西哥麵包	Mexican Sweet Rolls	79
咖哩麵包	Curry Buns	81
洋蔥培根麵包	Onion-Bacon Knots	83
菠蘿麵包	Rolls with Scaly Crust	85
全麥麵包	Whole Wheat Bread	87
圓頂奶油吐司	Domed Top Tin Loaf	89
圓頂葡萄乾吐司	Raisin Tin Loaf	91
五峰山形白吐司	Hilly Loaf	93

器皿介紹 : Introduction of Tools

麵刀
flour cutter

刮板
rubber specular

擠花袋
piping bag

花嘴
flowering mouth tube

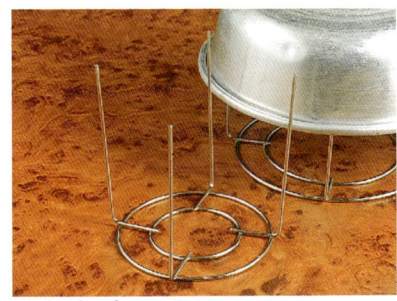
蛋糕插架
cake hanger

打蛋器
eletric mixer

吐司模
loaf tin

檸檬模
lemon mold

海綿蛋糕模
sponge cake mold

菊花模
chrysanthemum mold

乳酪蛋糕模
cheese cake mold

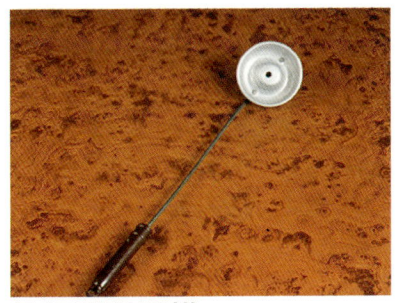
長柄甜甜圈模
doughnut mode

材料介紹：Introduction of Ingredients

新鮮酵母
active yeast

乾酵母
active dry yeast

ester s p

奶油霜
butter cream

起司
cheese

瑪琪琳酥片
sheet margarine

奶油
butter

酥油
butter oil substitute

瑪琪琳
margarine

白油
shortening

泡打粉
baking powder

塔塔粉
cream of tartar

可可粉
coca powder

濃縮柳橙汁
condense orange juice

巧克力米
chocolate rice

巧克力豆
chocolate chip

吉利丁
gelatin

麵粉的介紹

麵粉種類依蛋白質含量分類如下：

類　　別	蛋 白 質（%）	適 用 範 圍
高筋麵粉	11.5% 以上	麵包、吐司、甜甜圈、三角鬆餅
中筋麵粉	9.5% 以上	派皮、鳳梨酥、油皮、塔皮、核桃酥
低筋麵粉	6.5% 以上	月餅、泡芙、蛋糕、小西餅

Introduction of Flours

Flours are differentiated into three categories by their protein content:

Name	Protein {%}	Used for:
(bread flour) high gluten flour	11.5% and up	bread, tin loaves, doughnuts, deltas
(all-purpose flour) medium gluten flour	9.5% and up	pie shells, pineapple pastries, tart shells, water shortening dough, walnut pastries
(cake flour) low gluten flour	6.5% and up	cakes, cookies, moon cakes, puffs

奶油小西餅 Butter Fingers

奶油小西餅
Butter Fingers

| 奶油、糖粉 | 各90公克 | 蛋 | 2個 |
| 鹽 | ⅛小匙 | | |

1- ┌ 低筋麵粉 90公克
   │ 高筋麵粉 45公克
   └ 香草精 1小匙

1 烤箱預熱至１６０℃；烤盤抹油並撒上一層薄麵粉；蛋打成蛋液；低筋麵粉、高筋麵粉、糖粉分別過篩備用。
2 奶油用打蛋器打至呈淡黃色後，入糖粉、鹽打至變白，再將蛋液分次加入拌勻，最後入 **1** 料輕輕拌勻成麵糊。
3 將麵糊放入擠花袋內，擠成 7 公分長條，入烤箱上層烤10分鐘後，移至下層續烤3分鐘即可。

3 oz. (90 g) each: butter , powdered sugar
2 eggs
⅛ t. salt

1- ┌ **3½ oz. (90 g) cake flour**
   │ **1½ oz. (45 g) bread flour**
   └ **1 t. vanilla extract**

1 Preheat oven to 160°C (320°F). Grease and flour a baking sheet. Beat the eggs. Sift cake flour, bread flour, and sugar separately.
2 Beat butter until color turns light, add sugar and salt; beat until whiten. Beat in eggs a little at a time. Mix in **1** gently to become the batter.
3 Pour the batter into a piping bag and pipe the batter into 7 cm (3.5") strips on the baking sheet. Bake for 10 minutes on the upper rack of oven, then move the baking sheet to the low rack and bake for 3 more minutes.

花生醬小餅
Peanut Butter Cookies

| 低筋麵粉 | 170公克 | 糖粉 | 120公克 |
| 奶油、花生醬 | 各75公克 | 蛋 | 1個 |

1 烤箱預熱至１７０℃；烤盤刷油；低筋麵粉、糖粉分別過篩。
2 奶油置室溫下軟化，再加糖粉、花生醬混合用打蛋器打至鬆發後，加蛋拌勻，最後將低筋麵粉加入拌勻成糰，分成４０等份置於烤盤上。
3 圓形模型底部抹油，再將每份麵糰均勻壓平，放入烤箱烤１０分鐘即可。

6 oz. (170 g) cake flour
4¼ oz. (120 g) powdered sugar
2½ oz. (75 g) each: butter, peanut butter
1 egg

1 Preheat oven to 170°C (340°F). Grease a baking sheet. Sift flour and sugar, separately.
2 Soften butter at room temperature. Cream butter, sugar, and peanut butter in an electric mixer until fluffy. Add in the egg and fold in the flour; mix into a dough. Divide the dough into 40 equal parts and place on the greased baking sheet.
3 Grease the bottom of a round cookie mold. Flatten evenly each cookie dough with the mold. Bake for 10 minutes.

花生醬小餅 Peanut Butter Cookies

奶油椰子小西餅 Coconut Butter Cookies

奶油椰子小西餅
Coconut Butter Cookies

| 奶油 .... 250 公克 | 蛋 .... 25 公克 |
| 細砂糖、椰子粉 各 .. 125公克 | 蛋黃 .... 1 個 |

1⎡ 低筋麵粉 .... 350 公克
　⎣ 泡打粉 .... 1 小匙

1. 烤箱預熱至１８０℃；**1** 料混合過篩備用。
2. 奶油用打蛋器打至淡黃色後，入細砂糖拌勻，再分別入蛋、椰子粉拌勻，最後入 **1** 料輕輕拌壓均勻成麵糰（不可出筋），置冰箱冷藏１小時。
3. 取出麵糰，上下舖塑膠袋，用擀麵棍擀成０．３公分薄片，再用模型壓成小圓片後，置於烤盤上，表面刷上蛋黃液（可裝飾櫻桃在正中心），入烤箱上層烤 20 分鐘即可。

8¾ oz. (250 g) butter
4¾ oz. (125 g) each: granulated sugar, coconut powder
1 oz. (25 g) egg , beaten
1 egg yolk

1⎡ 12⅓ oz. (350 g) cake flour
　⎣ 1 t. baking powder

1. Preheat oven to 180°C (355°F). Sift **1**.
2. Cream the butter until color turns pale , mix in sugar, then add egg and coconut powder. Gently press in **1** (do not knead). Rest in refrigerator for one hour.
3. Place the dough on a plastic sheet and cover with a plastic sheet to prevent sticking, roll out the dough to a 0.3 cm (0.15") sheet. Cut the cookies out with a cookie mold. Brush with beaten egg yolk (maybe decorated with cherries). Bake on the upper rack of oven for 20 minutes.

脆皮花生小西餅
Peanut Macaroons

| 去皮花生 .... 400 公克 | 可可粉 .... 10 公克 |

1⎡ 蛋白 .... 3 個
　⎣ 細砂糖 .... 200 公克

1. 烤箱預熱至１７０℃備用。
2. 烤盤上置花生烤至金黃色後，取出用擀麵棍壓碎。
3. **1** 料打至輕微鬆發後，續入壓碎之花生拌勻，置爐火上加熱至呈濃稠拔絲狀即可離火，再入可可粉拌勻待涼，用湯匙舀盛在烤盤上成尖椎狀（共４０份），入烤箱烤２５分鐘即可。

14 oz. (400 g) skinned peanuts
⅓ oz. (10 g) cocoa powder

1⎡ 3 egg whites
　⎣ 7 oz. (200 g) granulated sugar

1. Preheat oven to 170°C (340° F).
2. Roast the peanuts until golden. Remove from oven and crush the peanuts with a rolling pin.
3. Beat **1** until fluffy, mix in the crushed peanuts. Heat over the stove until the mixture thickens to be toffee-like. Remove from the heat. Mix in the cocoa powder and leave to cool. Spoon onto the baking sheet (makes 40). Bake in the oven for 25 minutes.

脆皮花生小西餅 Peanut Macaroons

巧克力小餅 · Chocolate Cookies

糖粉	175公克
奶油	135公克
腰果	20粒
鹽	¼小匙
蛋	1個
❶ 低筋麵粉	200公克
可可粉	30公克
泡打粉	½小匙

1. 烤箱預熱至170℃；烤盤刷油❶料混合過篩；腰果從中一分為二備用（圖1）。
2. 奶油置室溫下軟化，加糖粉用打蛋器打至奶油顏色變淡時（圖2），加蛋拌勻，續加❶料及鹽混合成糊，分成40等份置於烤盤上。
3. 圓形模型底部抹油，將每份麵糊均勻壓平（圖3），上面以腰果裝飾，再入烤箱烤10分鐘即可。

6 oz. (175 g) powdered sugar
¼ oz. (135 g) .... butter
¼ t. .... salt
1 .... egg

❶ 7 oz. (200 g) cake flour
1 oz. (30 g) .... cocoa powder
½ t. ..... baking powder

1. Preheat oven to 170°C (340°F). Grease a baking sheet. Mix and sift ❶. Split each cashew nuts into halves (illus.1).
2. Soften the butter at room temperature. Cream butter and sugar in an electric mixer until fluffy and pale (illus. 2). Add the egg and mix well. Fold in ❶ and salt then mix into a smooth dough. Divide the dough into 40 small balls and place them on a greased baking sheet.
3. Grease the bottom of a round cookie mold. Flatten evenly each ball into a cookie (illus. 3). Decorate with cashew nuts. Bake for 10 minutes.

葡萄乾燕麥紅糖小西餅 · Oatmeal-Raisin Cookies

奶油	100公克
香草精	1小匙
蛋	2個

1
- 紅糖 60公克
- 細砂糖 40公克

2
- 葡萄乾 150公克
- 巧克力碎片 50公克
- 碎核桃 50公克

3
- 即食燕麥片 150公克
- 低筋麵粉 100公克
- 小蘇打 1/2小匙
- 鹽 1/2小匙

1 烤箱預熱至１６０℃；烤盤鋪上抗黏布（圖１）；蛋打散備用。
2 奶油置室溫下軟化，入**1**料拌勻，再入香草精攪拌後；將蛋液分次加入拌勻（圖２），續入**2**料攪拌，最後入**3**料輕輕拌勻，分成４０個小圓餅置於烤盤上（圖３），入烤箱烤１８分鐘即可。

3 1/2 oz. (100 g) .... butter
1 t. .... vanilla extract
2 .... eggs

1
- 2 1/3 oz. (60 g) .... brown sugar
- 1 1/3 oz. (40 g) .... granulated sugar

2
- 5 1/3 oz. (150 g) ... raisin
- 1 2/3 oz. (50 g) chocolate chips
- 1 2/3 oz. (50 g) . chopped walnuts

3
- 5 1/3 oz. (150 g) oatmeal
- 3 1/2 oz. (100 g) ...... cake flour
- 1/2 t. .... baking soda
- 1/2 t. .... salt

1 Preheat oven to 160°C (320°F). Line the baking sheet with grease proof paper (illus. 1). Beat the eggs.
2 Soften the butter at room temperature; mix well with **1**, add in vanilla. Beat in the eggs a little at a time (illus. 2). Stir in **2**, then mix in **3** gently. Divide into 40 small cookies and place on the baking sheet (illus. 3). Bake for 18 minutes.

擠花小西餅 · Piped Cookies

低筋麵粉	160 公克
奶油	130 公克
糖粉	70 公克
高筋麵粉	40 公克
奶水	30 公克
奶粉	20 公克
起司粉	10 公克
蛋	1 個
鹽	1/8 小匙

1 烤箱預熱至１７０℃；烤盤刷油；低筋麵粉、糖粉、高筋麵粉分別過篩備用。
2 奶油置室溫下軟化，加糖粉及鹽用打蛋器打至輕微鬆發後（圖1），再加蛋拌成糊狀，續入奶粉、起司粉、高筋麵粉、低筋麵粉輕輕拌勻（不可過份攪拌，以免出筋），最後入奶水拌勻並放入擠花袋中（用八牙花嘴圖2），擠在烤盤上（圖3），入烤箱烤１５分鐘即可。

5 1/2 oz. (160 g) .. cake flour
4 1/2 oz. (130 g) .... butter
2 1/3 oz. (70 g) .... powdered sugar
1 1/3 oz. (40 g) .. bread flour
2T. .... evaporated milk
2/3 oz. (20 g) .. milk powder
1/3 oz. (10 g) .... grated Parmesan cheese
1 .... egg
1/8 t. .... salt

1 Preheat oven to 170°C (340°F). Grease a baking sheet. Sift cake flour, sugar, bread flour, separately.
2 Soften the butter at room temperature. Cream the butter, sugar, and salt in a electric mixer until fluffy (illus.1); beat in the egg. Mix in milk powder, grated Parmesan cheese, bread flour, and cake flour; gently mix well (do not over stir to prevent hardening). Stir in the milk and mix evenly. Pour the batter into a piping bag (with a flowering mouth tube, illus.2). Pipe directly onto the greased baking sheet (illus.3). Bake for 15 minutes.

蛋黃小西餅 · Cookie Sandwiches

低筋麵粉	180公克
糖粉	150公克
蛋黃	4個
蛋	2個
糖粉、奶油霜	適量
1 氨粉、香草精、鹽	各½小匙

1. 烤箱預熱至200℃；烤盤刷油並撒上一層薄麵粉；低筋麵粉、糖粉分別過篩備用。
2. 蛋、蛋黃、糖粉混合用打蛋器打發後，續打至糊狀，再入 **1** 料及低筋麵粉拌勻成麵糊，放進擠花袋中（用平口花嘴）（圖1），擠直徑3公分的圓形，並在表面撒上少許糖粉（圖2），入烤箱烤6分鐘後，取出待涼。
3. 取兩片餅乾，底層均勻塗上奶油霜（圖3），再合併起來，依序作完即可。

6⅓ oz. (180 g) cake flour
5⅓ oz. (150 g) powdered sugar
4 .... egg yolks
2 .... eggs
as needed powdered sugar, butter cream

1 ½ t. each: Hartshorn salt (or double quantity of baking powder) vanilla extract, salt

1. Preheat oven to 200 °C (390 °F). Grease a baking sheet and dust on a thin layer of flour. Sift flour and sugar, separately.
2. Cream the eggs, egg yolks, and sugar in a mixer until smooth. Add **1** and flour, mix until forms a smooth dough. Place into a piping bag (with a even mouth illus. 1), squeeze the dough into 3 cm (1.5") diameter cookies; dust with a dash of powdered sugar (illus. 2). Bake in the oven for six minutes. Remove and let them cool.
3. Spread the bottom of each cookie with butter cream (illus. 3). Stick two cookies together to be a cookie sandwich.

冰箱小西餅 · Refrigerator Cookies

低筋麵粉	300公克
糖粉	270公克
奶油	210公克
起司粉	60公克
可可粉	25公克
蛋	1個
奶水	1/4杯

1. 烤箱預熱至１８０℃；低筋麵粉、糖粉、可可粉分別過篩備用。
2. 糖粉加軟化之奶油打發至奶油顏色變淡後，入蛋拌勻，再入起司粉及低筋麵粉拌勻，最後入奶水1/4杯拌勻成白麵糰，分成９份。
3. 取一份白麵糰擀成大薄片，再取 4 份白麵糰分別加入可可粉揉成可可麵糰，然後將剩餘之白麵糰和可可麵糰分別搓成細長條備用。
4. 在大薄片之白麵糰上刷少許奶水，上置可可及白麵條，相間排列後（圖 1），再刷上奶水（圖２），上面再放上相間排列之可可及白麵條，然後將大薄片包捲成長條狀（圖３），裝入塑膠袋中置冰箱冷凍堅硬，取出，切０·３公分厚薄片，入烤箱烤１０分鐘即可。

10½ oz. (300 g) cake flour
9½ oz. (270 g) .. powdered sugar
7½ oz. (210 g) .... butter
2⅓ oz. (60 g) .... grated Parmesan cheese
1 oz. (25 g) cocoa powder
1 .... egg
¼ C. ...... evaporated milk

1. Preheat oven to 180°C (355°F). Sift flour, powdered sugar, cocoa, separately.
2. Cream soft butter with sugar until light and fluffy, beat in the egg. Then add in Parmesan cheese and cake flour, mix well. Pour in ¼ C. evaporated milk and mix well. This is the white dough. Divide the white dough into 9 equal portions.
3. Roll out a portion of white dough into a big thin sheet. Mix cocoa powder into the other 4 portions of white dough to become 4 cocoa doughs, Roll 4 cocoa doughs and the remaining 4 white doughs into long logs.
4. Brush a little milk on the white dough sheet, then place cocoa and white dough on top (illus. 1). Brush another layer of milk on (illus. 2). Place another layer of cocoa and white dough on the top. Roll them up (illus. 3) into a cylinder, and wrap in a plastic bag. Freeze until hard. Cut logs into slices 0.3cm (0.15") thick and bake for 10 minutes.

巧克力白帽小西餅 · Snow-Capped Cook Sandwiches

沙拉油	20 公克
糖粉	1/2 杯

1
- 細砂糖 .... 75 公克
- 白油 .... 25 公克
- 可可粉 .... 10 公克
- 奶粉 .... 2 公克
- 鹽、香草精 .... 各 1/4 小匙

2
- 蛋 .... 1 個
- 氨粉 .... 1/8 小匙

3
- 低筋麵粉 .... 75 公克
- 泡打粉 .... 1/4 小匙

1. 烤箱預熱至 180℃；**3**料及糖粉分別過篩備用。
2. **1**料用攪拌器拌勻，慢慢加入沙拉油，再入**2**料充分拌勻，最後入**3**料拌成濃稠狀麵糊（圖1），置冰箱冷藏2小時以上，取出搓成小球狀（圖2），放入糖粉內沾裹一層糖粉後（圖3），置於烤盤上，入烤箱烤10分鐘後，取出待涼。
3. 取兩片餅乾，底層均勻塗上奶油霜，再合併起來，依序作完即可。

- 3/4 oz. (20 g) .... salad oil
- 1/2 C. .... powdered sugar

1
- 2 2/3 oz. (75 g) .... granulated sugar
- 1 oz. (25 g) shortening
- 1/3 oz. (10 g) .... cocoa powder
- 1/2 t. .... milk powder
- 1/4 t. each: salt, vanilla extract

2
- 1 .... egg
- 1/8 t. ..... Hartshorn salt

3
- 2 2/3 oz. (75 g) cake flour
- 1/4 t. .... baking powder

1. Preheat oven to 180°C (355°F). Sift **3** and powdered sugar, separately.
2. Beat **1** in a mixer until well-mixed. Add salad oil a little at a time and then add **2** and beat well. Add **3** and mix into a thick batter (illus.1). Place the batter in the refrigerator to chill for two hours. Roll the batter into small balls (illus.2). Dip the tip into powdered sugar (illus.3) Place them on a baking sheet and bake for 10 minutes. Remove from the oven and leave to cool.
3. Sandwich two cookies together with a layer of butter cream.

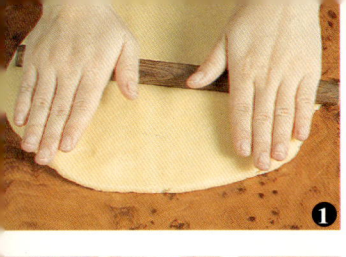

營養餅乾 · Nutritious Biscuits

低筋麵粉	300公克
細砂糖	80公克
奶油	50公克
蛋	2個
鹽、泡打粉	各½小匙

❶ 蛋黃 1個
　 椰子粉 2小匙

1　烤箱預熱至160℃；低筋麵粉、泡打粉過篩；奶油溶化成液態；❶料混合拌勻備用。

2　細砂糖加蛋、鹽拌勻至糖溶化，再入奶油、低筋麵粉、泡打粉揉成光滑麵糰，放置鬆弛30分鐘後，擀成0.3公分薄片（圖1）。另用圓形印模將薄片切割成圓狀（圖2），再用叉子在上面刺洞後，將❶料刷在餅乾表面（圖3），入烤箱烤20分鐘即可。

10½ oz. (300 g) cake flour
2¾ oz. (80 g) ... granulated sugar
1⅔ oz. (50 g) .... butter
2 .... eggs
½ t. each: salt, baking powder

❶ 1 egg yolk
　 2 t. coconut powder

1　Preheat oven to 160°C (320°F). Sift cake flour and baking powder. Melt the butter or margarine. Mix ❶ well for later use.

2　Mix sugar, eggs, and salt until sugar dissolves; add in butter or margarine, cake flour, and baking powder. Knead the mixture into a smooth dough. Let it rest for 30 minutes. Roll out dough to a 0.3 cm (0.15") thin sheet (illus. 1), and cut out the biscuits with a round cookie cutter (illus. 2). Prick the surface with a fork, and brush with ❶ (illus. 3). Bake in an oven for 20 minutes.

葡萄酥 · Oblong Raisin Bars

低筋麵粉	250公克
蛋	1個
蛋黃	1個
葡萄乾、奶油、糖粉	各100公克

1. 烤箱預熱至１８０℃；烤盤刷油。
2. 葡萄乾泡水５分鐘再洗去糖份，瀝乾水份（圖１）；低筋麵粉、糖粉分別過篩備用。
3. 奶油置室溫下軟化，加糖粉用打蛋器打至奶油變淡黃色，再將蛋放入拌勻，續入葡萄乾拌勻，最後入低筋麵粉輕輕揉成糰，分成３０等份。
4. 將每份麵糰搓成橄欖形（圖２），置於烤盤上，表面刷上蛋黃液（圖３），入烤箱烤２０分鐘至表面呈金黃色即可。

9 oz. (250 g) cake flour
3½ oz. (100 g) each : raisins, butter or margarine, powdered sugar
1 .... egg
1 .... egg yolk

1. Preheat oven to 180°C (355°F). Grease a baking sheet.
2. Soak the raisins in water for 5 minutes and wash off the sugar, drain (illus. 1). Sift flour and sugar, separately.
3. Soften the butter at room temperature. Cream the butter and sugar in a mixer until light and fluffy; add in the egg and mix well. Add in the raisins. Add the flour and gently knead into a dough. Divide the dough into 30 equal portions.
4. Knead each portion into a oblong olive shape bun (illus. 2), place on the baking sheet. Brush the surface with beatened egg yolk (illus. 3). Bake in the oven for 20 minutes or until golden.

杏仁酥條 · Almond Bars

低筋麵粉	....	200 公克
杏仁片	....	130 公克
奶油	....	35 公克
1｛ 奶油	....	115 公克
糖粉	....	85 公克
鹽	....	1/8 小匙
2｛ 蛋黃	....	1 個
奶水	....	2 大匙
3｛ 細砂糖	....	70 公克
蛋白	....	1 個

1. 烤箱預熱至１８０℃；低筋麵粉、糖粉分別過篩備用。
2. **1**料打發成淡黃色，再入**2**料拌成糊狀後，入低筋麵粉拌壓成糰，置冰箱冷藏３０分鐘使之鬆弛。
3. 取出麵糰鋪在烤盤上，用手壓平且厚度均勻（圖１），入烤箱烤１５分鐘取出。
4. **3**料打發至輕微起泡，再隔水加熱（圖２）煮至糖溶化後，取出，將奶油放入溶解，最後入杏仁片隔水加熱煮至拔絲狀（約３分鐘）（圖３）即可離火。
5. 將煮好的杏仁片均勻鋪在麵皮上，入１５０℃烤箱烤至表面上色後（約１５分鐘），取出趁熱翻面，切成５公分長條狀即可。

7 oz. (200 g) ..... cake flour
4 1/2 oz. (130 g) .... almond slices
1 1/3 oz. (35 g) .... butter

1｛ 4 oz. (115 g) ...... butter
3 oz.(85 g) .. powdered sugar
1/8 t. .... salt

2｛ 1 .... egg yolk
2T. ... evaporated milk

3｛ 2 1/3 oz. (70 g) .... granulated sugar
1 .... egg white

1. Preheat oven to 180°C (355°F). Sift flour and sugar, separately.
2. Cream **1** until light and fluffy, add in **2** and mix into a paste. Add flour and knead into a dough. Rest the dough in refrigerator for 30 minutes.
3. Place the dough on a baking sheet, press down by hand to a block with even thickness (illus. 1). Bake for 15 minutes. Remove.
4. Beat **3** until slightly foamy, heat over water (illus. 2) until sugar has melted, remove. Melt butter in the warm sugar syrup, add in almond slices. Again heat over water until it becomes toffee-like (about 3 minutes) (illus. 3). Remove from heat.
5. Spread the candied almond slices over the bread, bake in 150°C (300°F) oven until the surface nicely colored (about 15 minutes). Remove from the baking sheet while still warm. Cut into 5 cm (2 ") long bars.

起司酥條 · Cheese-filled Rolls

酥皮：奶油 80公克

① 中筋麵粉 200公克
　 糖粉 20公克

② 冰水 1/3杯
　 鹽 1/8小匙

餡：低筋麵粉 60公克
　　奶水、蛋黃 各1大匙

③ 起司片 200公克
　 細砂糖 40公克

1　烤箱預熱至１８０℃；① 料及低筋麵粉分別過篩備用。
2　奶油切成小塊置室溫下軟化後，入 ① 料，以切成小塊狀的方式使麵粉和奶油拌勻（圖１），續入 ② 料拌揉成光滑麵糰，以塑膠袋密封，置冰箱冷藏３０分鐘即為酥皮。
3　③ 料隔水加熱煮至糊狀後離火，再入低筋麵粉拌揉成糰即為起司餡，將之搓成１５公分之長條２份備用。
4　取1/2 酥皮擀成１５×１０公分之片狀，刷上少許奶水（圖２），再將起司餡置於其上（圖３），並將麵皮包捲成圓柱狀後，搓成約６０公分之細長條，再切成３段置於烤盤上，表面刷上蛋黃並用牙籤在表面劃細條紋，另一份也依此方法做好後，入烤箱烤２５分鐘，取出待涼切成適當長度即可。

Pastry: 2 3/4 oz. (80 g) .... butter or margarine

① 7 oz. (200 g) .... all purpose flour
　 2/3 oz. (20 g) powdered sugar

② 1/3 C. .... ice water
　 1/8 t. .... salt

Filling: 2 1/4 oz. (60 g) cake flour
1 T. each: evaporated milk, egg yolk

③ 7 oz. (200 g) .. cheddar cheese
　 1 1/3 oz. (40 g) .... granulated sugar

1　Preheat oven to 180 °C (355 °F). Sift separately ① and cake flour.
2　Cube the butter or margarine and leave them to soften at room temperature, mix with ①(illus. 1). Add ② and knead to a smooth dough. Seal with plastic bag and let it rest in refrigerator for 30 minutes. This is the pastry dough.
3　Heat ③ over water until melted, remove from heat. Mix in cake flour and knead to be the cheese filling. Knead the filling into two 15 cm (6") long strips.
4　Roll half of the pastry dough out to be a 15 cm x 10 cm (6"x4") sheet, brush on a little evaporated milk (illus. 2). Place one cheese filling strip in the center (illus. 3), roll it up like a cylinder and knead it into a 60 cm (24") long thin strip. Cut the strip into 3 sections. Brush the surface with egg yolk and score the surface with a toothpick. Repeat the same with the other half of the pastrydough. Bake in an oven for 25 minutes. Remove and leave them to cool. Cut into serving pieces.

蝴蝶酥 · Butterfly Pastries

瑪琪琳酥片	340公克
細砂糖	100公克

1
- 高筋麵粉 200公克
- 低筋麵粉 75公克
- 蛋 1個
- 冰水 1/2杯
- 鹽 1/4小匙

1. 烤箱預熱至２００℃；高筋、低筋麵粉混和過篩備用。
2. **1**料全部混合揉成光滑麵糊，放置鬆弛１５分鐘後，包入瑪琪琳酥片，再擀成０．３公分厚長方形薄片（圖１），由兩邊拉起對疊至中心處（圖２），使麵糊變成兩層，再對疊成四層（圖３），置冰箱冷藏鬆弛２０分鐘，如此重覆４次即成酥皮。
3. 酥皮擀成寬２０公分、厚０．３公分之長方形，並於兩面均勻撒上細砂糖後，由兩邊拉起對疊至中心處，使麵糊變成兩層，再對疊成四層後，續對疊成八層，置冰箱冷藏鬆弛３０分鐘，再切成０．６公分寬長條，平放置於烤盤上，入烤箱烤１２分鐘，翻面再烤８分鐘即可。

---

12 oz. (340 g) .... sheet margarine
3 1/2 oz. (100 g) . granulated sugar

1
- 7 oz. (200 g) ...... bread flour
- 2 1/2 oz.(75 g) .... cake flour
- 1 .... egg
- 1/2 C. .... ice water
- 1/4 t. .... salt

1. Preheat oven to 200°C (390°F). Mix bread flour and cake flour; sift.
2. Mix all the ingredients in **1** and knead into a smooth dough. Let it rest for 15 minutes. Fold in sheet margarine. Roll out dough to 0.3 cm(0.15") thick rectangular sheet (illus. 1). Pull two sides up and fold them to the center (illus. 2), now the dough becomes two layered. Fold again to become four layered (illus. 3). Rest in refrigerator for 20 minutes. Repeat the process 4 times. This is the puff pastry dough.
3. Roll out the dough to 20 cm (8 ") wide, 0.3 cm (0.15") thick rectangular roll. Dust both sides with granulated sugar. Pull the sides up and fold them to the center, now the dough again is two layered. Fold again to 4 layers, again to 8 layers. Rest in refrigerator for 30 minutes. Cut into 0.6 cm (0.3") wide strips. Place on a baking sheet and bake for 12 minutes. Turn over and bake for 8 minutes.

空心泡芙 Basic Puffs

鮮蝦泡芙
Prawn Salad Puffs

| 空心泡芙 | 24 個 | 大蝦仁 | 24 條 |

1
- 馬鈴薯 .... 180 公克
- 小黃瓜 .... 90 公克
- 胡蘿蔔 .... 80 公克

2
- 沙拉醬 .... 125 公克
- 玉米粒 .... 50 公克
- 白煮蛋（切丁）....... 1 個

1 蝦仁去腸泥洗淨後，劃開背部，入開水中燙熟撈出備用。
2 **1**料切細丁入開水中燙熟，取出待涼後，入**2**料拌勻，填入空心泡芙中，頂端再放上一隻蝦仁並蓋上切下之泡芙皮即可。

24 basic puffs
24 prawns

1
- 6¹/₃ oz. (180 g) potatoes
- 3 oz. (90 g) baby cucumbers
- 2³/₄ oz. (80 g) carrots

2
- 4¹/₂ oz. (125 g) mayonnaise
- 1²/₃ oz. (50 g) corn
- 1 diced hard-boiled egg

1 Wash and devein the prawns; slit open the backs and cook in boiling water until done. Remove and drain.
2 Dice **1**, cook in boiling water until done; remove and leave them to cool. Mix with **2**. Cut a lid off the puffs. Fill with the salad and top with a prawn. Replace the lids and serve.

空心泡芙
Basic Puffs

| 低筋麵粉 .... 125 公克 | 蛋 .... 5 個 |

1
- 水 .... 175 公克
- 酥油 .... 125 公克

1 烤箱預熱至１８０℃；烤盤抹油並灑上一層薄麵粉備用。
2 **1**料置鋼盆中煮滾（約１０４℃，邊煮邊攪拌）（圖1），再入過篩之低筋麵粉拌勻後（圖2）熄火，趁熱依序加蛋拌勻（一次一個蛋，拌勻後才可再加蛋）（圖3），待不燙手時，裝入擠花袋中（圖4）擠在烤盤上（圖5）（共２４個），再入烤箱烤２０分鐘，取出待涼即可（圖6）。

4¹/₂ oz. (125 g) cake flour
5 eggs

1
- ³/₄ C. water
- 4¹/₂ oz. (125 g) butter oil substitute

1 Preheat oven to 180 °C (355 °F). Grease a baking sheet and lightly dust on a layer of flour.
2 Bring **1** to a boil (about 104° C/210 °F, must stir constantly)(illus.1). Mix in sifted cake flour (illus.2) and turn off the heat. While still warm, add eggs (one at a time, beating well after each addition) (illus.3). When slightly cooled off, place the mixture into a piping bag.(illus.4) Pipe the puffs onto the baking sheet (makes 24).(illus.5) Bake in the oven for 20 minutes. Remove and allow to cool.(illus.6)

鮮蝦泡芙 Prawn Salad Puffs

火腿沙拉泡芙 Ham Salad Puffs

蒸烤雞蛋牛奶布丁
Caramel Pudding

鮮奶 .... 1000 公克(100%)　　蛋 .... 480 公克(48%)
細砂糖 .... 100 公克(10%)　　水 .... 100 公克(10%)

1　白砂糖 ..... 150 公克(15%)
　　　水 .... 50 公克(5%)

1　烤箱預熱至１５０℃；烤盤加水五分滿備用。
2　鮮奶與細砂糖拌勻，以中火煮至糖溶化後，待涼，入打勻之蛋液並過篩備用。
3　**1**料以小火煮至溶化且呈焦紅色，再入１００公克冷水煮開，倒入8寸空心圓模中冰涼使其凝固，續入作法2之材料後，置於烤盤中，入烤箱下層烤４０分鐘，再移至中層續烤20分鐘即可。

2¹/₅ lb. (1000 g) fresh milk (100%)
17 oz. (480 g) eggs (48%)
3¹/₂ oz. (100 g) granulated sugar (10%)
²/₅ C. water (10%)

1　5¹/₃ oz. (150 g) granulated sugar (15%)
　　　3¹/₃ T. (50 g) water (5%)

1　Preheat oven to 150 °C (300° F).
2　Mix milk and sugar, boil over medium heat until sugar dissolves; cool completely. Add in beaten eggs and sieve the mixture through a colander.
3　Heat **1** over low heat until caramelized to brownish red. Add 100 g (3¹/₂ oz.) cold water into the caramel and bring to a boil. Pour the caramel into a 8" ring mold and leave to set. Pour the egg mixture on top of the set caramel and place in a pan of water, bake on the low rack of the oven for 40 minutes. Then bake at the center of the oven for 20 more minutes.

火腿沙拉泡芙
Ham Salad Puffs

空心泡芙 .... 24 個

1　西芹丁、沙拉醬 ....
　　　................. 各150 公克
　　　蘋果丁 .... 120 公克
　　　洋火腿丁 .... 80 公克

1　西芹丁入開水中燙熟後，取出漂涼。
2　**1**料拌勻，填入切開之空心泡芙中，再蓋上切下之泡芙皮即可。

24 basic puffs

1　5¹/₃ oz. (150 g) each: diced celery, mayonnaise
　　　4¹/₃ oz. (120 g) diced apple
　　　2¹/₃ oz. (80 g) diced ham

1　Parboil diced celery and rinse under cold water to cool. Remove.
2　Mix **1** well to be the filling. Cut a lid off each puff and fill. Replace the lids.

蒸烤雞蛋牛奶布丁 Caramel Pudding

咖啡愛克力 · Coffee Eclairs

空心泡芙材料1份（見第23頁）奶油布丁餡材料1份（見第26頁）
即溶咖啡粉 .... 1 大匙
杏仁片 100公克

1⎡ 即溶咖啡粉（再壓成粉末狀）........................ 2 小匙
  ⎣ 巧克力 100公克

1. 空心泡芙材料拌勻後，在烤盤上擠成長條狀（圖1），其餘作法與空心泡芙相同，烤出來之成品即為愛克力空心泡芙。
2. 咖啡奶油布丁餡：
鮮奶與即溶咖啡粉拌勻後，再加糖煮開，其餘作法與奶油布丁餡作法相同。(參見第26頁)
3. 杏仁片入200℃烤箱烤至表面呈金黃色備用。
4. 愛克力空心泡芙橫切開後，填入咖啡奶油布丁餡（圖2），再蓋上愛克力空心泡芙皮，另**1**料隔水加熱煮化後，淋在咖啡愛克力上，最後也可灑上杏仁片裝飾（圖3）。

1 full quantity of Basic Puffs materials (ref.pg.23)
1 full quantity of cream filling for puffs (ref.pg.26)
1 T. instant coffee powder
3½ oz. (100 g) .... almond slices

1⎡ 2 t. instant coffee powder (must pound to fine powder)
  ⎣ 3½ oz.(100 g) chocolate

1. Prepare the dough as directed in "Basic Puffs". Pipe the dough in long strips onto the baking sheet (illus. 1). Bake as directed in" Basic Puffs".
2. Coffee cream filling:
Mix fresh milk with instant coffee powder, add sugar and bring to a boil. Contine as recipe for cream filling. (ref. pg.26)
3. Roast almond slices in preheated 200 °C (390 °F) oven until golden.
4. Cut a lid off each puff, fill with the coffee cream filling (illus. 2). Replace the lids. Boil **1** over water, ice the pastries and you may decorate with almond slices (illus. 3).

奶油泡芙 · Cream Filled Puffs

空心泡芙	24個
鮮奶	1000公克
細砂糖	188公克
奶油	75公克
⓵ 玉米粉	150公克
蛋	5個

1. 鮮奶加細砂糖煮開後，趁熱沖入拌勻之 ⓵ 中攪拌均勻，再置於爐火上，邊加熱邊攪拌至呈濃稠狀後，熄火，入奶油拌勻即為奶油布丁餡，待涼備用。
2. 將空心泡芙橫切開1/3後，填入奶油布丁餡，再蓋上切下之泡芙皮即可。

■ 鮮奶油水果泡芙：作法與奶油泡芙相同，但在填入奶油布丁餡後，可放上水果，並擠上打發之鮮奶油作裝飾。

■ 天鵝泡芙：作法與奶油泡芙相同，但切下之空心泡芙蓋子再一切為二當天鵝之翅膀（圖1），另外用細孔花嘴擠細長s形麵糊（圖2）烤熟當脖子，另用溶化之巧克力點出天鵝眼睛，並用打發之鮮奶油擠在天鵝尾巴當裝飾即可（圖3）。

24	basic puffs
4 1/5 C.	fresh milk
6 2/3 oz.(188 g)	granulated sugar
2 2/3 oz. (75 g)	butter or margarine
⓵ 5 1/3 oz. (150 g)	corn flour
5	eggs

1. Bring milk and sugar to a boil, pour into ⓵ while still warm; mix well. Place again over heat, stir constantly until thickens to paste. Remove from heat and mix in the butter or margarine. This is the custard cream filling. Leave it to cool.
2. Cut a lid off each puff, fill each with custard cream. Replace the lids.

■ Cream and fruit Puffs: After filling with the custard cream, decorate with fruits and whipped cream.

■ Swan Puffs: Cut the lids into halves as the swan wings (illus. 1). Pipe the dough into S-shaped strips (illus. 2) as the swan necks, bake until done. Dot the eyes with melted chocolate. Decorate the tails with whipped cream (illus. 3).

酵母甜甜圈 · Raised Doughnuts

高筋麵粉 300公克
乾酵母 6公克
細砂糖 .... 適量

❶ ⎡ 蛋液 60公克
　 ⎢ 細砂糖 36公克
　 ⎢ 奶粉 10公克
　 ⎣ 鹽 .... 3/8 小匙

❷ 瑪琪琳、白油 . 各27公克

1　乾酵母加水１２０公克溶解後，入拌勻之❶料中，即為酵母液。
2　高筋麵粉過篩後，入酵母液中並加❷料拌勻即為麵糊。
3　麵糊置室溫發酵約９０分鐘（膨發成２倍大），表面灑上少許高筋麵粉使麵糊不粘手（圖１），再擀成２公分厚之片狀，並以模型切成甜甜圈形狀後（圖２），繼續發酵３０分鐘即為酵母甜甜圈麵糊。
4　鍋熱入油６杯燒至１５０℃，入酵母甜甜圈以小火炸至兩面呈金黃色後，取出趁熱沾上細砂糖即可（圖３）。

■ 巧克力甜甜圈之作法與酵母甜甜圈相同，只要在❶料中多加１８公克之可可粉、水、細砂糖即可。

10 1/2 oz. (300 g) bread flour
1/5 oz. (6 g) active dry yeast
as needed granulated sugar

❶ ⎡ 2 oz. (60 g) ... beatened eggs
　 ⎢ 1 1/4 oz. (36 g) .... granulated sugar
　 ⎢ 1/3 oz. (10 g) .... milk powder
　 ⎣ 3/8 t. .... salt

❷ ⎡ 1 oz. (27 g) each: ....
　 ⎣ margarine, shortening

1　Dissolve the yeast in 120 g (4 1/4 oz.) water, and mix well with ❶. This is the yeast solution.
2　Sift bread flour and mix with yeast solution and ❷. This is the dough.
3　Let the dough stand at the room temperature to raise for 90 minutes (Double the size). Dust with a little bread flour (illus. 1) and roll it to 2 cm (1") thick sheet. Cut the doughnuts out with a doughnut cutter (illus. 2). Let them stand and rise for 30 minutes. They are raised dough doughnuts.
4　Heat the frying pot, add 6 C. oil and heat to 150°C (300°F). Deep fry the doughnuts over low heat until golden on both sides. Remove and dust on powdered sugar (illus. 3).

■ Chocolate Doughnuts: Add 2/3 oz. (18 g) each of cocoa powder, water, and granulated sugar into ❶. The rest remains the same.

馬鈴薯甜甜圈 · Potato Doughnuts

高筋麵粉 ..... 160公克(100％)
馬鈴薯 .... 100公克(62.5％)
低筋麵粉 .... 40公克(25％)
乾酵母 .... 8公克(5％)
細砂糖 .... 適量

1
細砂糖 .... 64公克(40％)
蛋液 .... 40公克(25％)
白油 .... 32公克(20％)
黃豆粉 .... 24公克(15％)
奶粉 .... 10公克(6.25％)
鹽 .... 1公克(0.625％)

1 馬鈴薯去皮煮熟，壓成泥狀備用。
2 **1**料以打蛋器攪勻，入馬鈴薯泥中拌勻。
3 乾酵母加水１１０公克溶解後，再入薯泥及過篩之高、低筋麵粉拌勻成麵糊。
4 麵糊置室溫發酵１小時（膨發成２倍大），表面灑上少許高筋麵粉使麵糊不粘手（圖１），再擀成２公分厚之片狀，並以模型切成甜甜圈形狀後（圖２），繼續發酵３０分鐘即為馬鈴薯多拿滋。
5 鍋熱入油６杯燒至１５０℃，入馬鈴薯多拿滋以小火炸至兩面呈金黃色後，取出趁熱沾上細砂糖即可（圖３）。

$5^{2}/_{3}$ oz.(160 g) .... bread flour(100％)
$3^{1}/_{2}$ oz.(100 g) .... potato(62.5％)
$1^{1}/_{2}$ oz. (40 g) .... cake flour(25％)
$^{1}/_{4}$ oz.(8 g) .... active dry yeast(5％)

1
$2^{1}/_{4}$ oz. (64 g) .... granulated sugar(40％)
$1^{1}/_{2}$ oz. (40 g) .... beatened eggs(25％)
$1^{1}/_{4}$ oz. (32 g) .... shortening(20％)
$^{3}/_{4}$ oz.(24 g) .... soy flour(15％)
$^{1}/_{3}$ oz. (10 g) .... milk powder(6.25％)
$^{1}/_{4}$ t. .... salt(0.625％)

1 Peel and boil potatoes; mash to paste.
2 Beat **1** well and mix with mashed potatoes.
3 Dissolve yeast in 110 g (3 $^{4}/_{5}$ oz.) water; add in potato mixture, sifted bread flour and sifted cake flour. Mix well.
4 Let the dough stand at room temperature to rise for one hour (To double the size). Dust the surface with a little bread flour (illus. 1), roll out to 2 cm (1") thick sheet. Cut out the doughnuts with doughnut cutter (illus. 2). Let them stand to rise again for 30 minutes.
5 Heat the frying pot, add 6 C. oil and heat to 150°C (300 °F). Deep fry doughnuts over low heat until golden on both sides. Sprinkle on granulated sugar while still warm (illus. 3).

豆沙甜甜圈 · Bean Paste Filled Doughnuts

豆沙 .... 120 公克
細砂糖 .... 適量

① ┌ 細砂糖 .... 88 公克
   └ 蛋 .... 2 個

② ┌ 沙拉油、奶水 ....
   └ .... 各25 公克

③ ┌ 低筋麵粉 .... 250 公克
   │ 泡打粉 .... 1 小匙
   └ 肉桂粉 .... ¼ 小匙

1. ❶料以打蛋器打至細砂糖完全溶解後（圖1），入❷料拌勻，再入過篩之❸料拌勻即為麵糊，入冰箱冷藏鬆弛20分鐘。
2. 豆沙每份分成5公克備用。
3. 取出麵糊，表面灑上少許高筋麵粉使麵糊不粘手（圖2），再分成每份20公克之小麵糊。
4. 將每份小麵糊擀平，包入豆沙捏成圓形（圖3），依序作完即為豆沙多拿滋。
5. 鍋熱入油6杯燒至120℃，入豆沙多拿滋以小火炸至表面呈金黃色後，取出趁熱沾上細砂糖即可。

4¼ oz. (120 g) .... red bean paste
as needed granulated sugar

① ┌ 3 oz. (88 g) granulated sugar
   └ 2 .... eggs

② ┌ 1 oz. (25 g) each: salad oil, evaporated milk

③ ┌ 9 oz. (250 g) cake flour
   │ 1 t. ...... baking powder
   └ ¼ t. cinnamon powder

1. Beat ❶ until sugar dissolves (illus. 1). Mix with ❷ and add in sifted ❸. Mix it well to be the dough. Rest in the refrigerator for 20 minutes.
2. Divide the red bean paste into ⅙ oz. (5 g) portions.
3. Dust the dough with a little bread flour (illus. 2) and divide into ¾ oz. (20 g) dough portions.
4. Roll each portion flat, wrap in a portion of red bean paste and roll into a small ball (illus. 3). Repeat until all done.
5. Heat a frying pot, add 6 C. oil and heat to 120 °C (250 °F). Deep fry the doughnuts over low heat until golden. While still warm, sprinkle on granulated sugar.

蛋糕甜甜圈 · Cake Doughnuts

細砂糖	適量
1 低筋麵粉	300公克
泡打粉	9公克
2 奶水	164公克
細砂糖	90公克
酥油	30公克
奶粉	18公克
黃豆粉	9公克
蛋	2個
香草精	1小匙
鹽	1/4小匙
荳蔻粉	1/8小匙

1. **1** 料過篩備用。
2. **2** 料拌勻後，入 **1** 料攪拌均勻即成麵糊，再入擠花袋中備用。
3. 鍋熱入油6杯燒至150℃，入長柄甜甜圈模型燒熱（圖1），再取出擠入麵糊（圖2），續入油鍋中以小火炸至定型後，取下模型續炸至兩面呈金黃色後，取出趁熱沾上細砂糖即可（圖3）。

---

as needed granulated sugar

1
- 10²⁄₃ oz. (300 g) .... cake flour
- ¹⁄₃ oz. (9 g) .... baking powder

2
- ³⁄₅ C. evaporated milk
- 3¹⁄₄ oz. (90 g) granulated sugar
- 1 oz. (30 g) .. butter oil substitute
- ²⁄₃ oz. (18 g) .... milk powder
- ¹⁄₃ oz. (9 g) .... soy flour
- 2 .... eggs
- 1 t. .... vanilla extract
- ¹⁄₄ t. .... salt
- ¹⁄₈ t. .... nutmeg

1. Sift **1**.
2. Mix **2**, add **1** and mix well to be the dough. Place the dough into a piping bag.
3. Heat a frying pot, add 6 C. oil and heat to 150 °C (300 °F). Lower the doughnut mode into the hot oil to heat (illus. 1). Lift out the mode and pipe the dough into the mode (illus. 2). Deep fry over low heat until the dough is set, then remove the mode. Continue frying to golden on both sides. While still hot, sprinkle on granulated sugar (illus. 3).

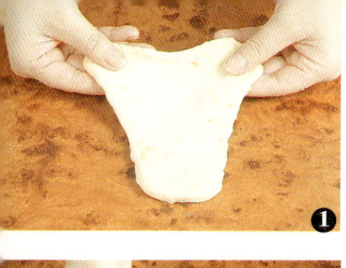

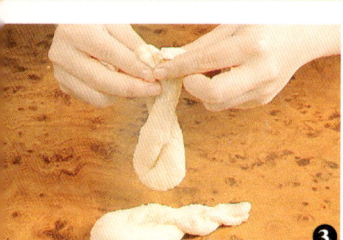

桔子麻花甜甜圈 · Orange Twisters

橘子(淨重)	150 公克
白油	75 公克
乾酵母	18 公克
細砂糖	適量

1
- 蛋 .... 100 公克
- 細砂糖 .... 75 公克
- 奶粉 .... 20 公克
- 鹽 .... 1 小匙

2
- 高筋麵粉 .... 350 公克
- 低筋麵粉 .... 150 公克
- 泡打粉 .... 1 小匙

1. 橘子去籽及膜後，用湯匙攪碎，入 **1** 料中拌勻備用。
2. 乾酵母加水３大匙溶解後，入作法１之材料及過篩之 **2** 料拌勻，再入白油攪拌均勻即為麵糰。
3. 麵糰置室溫發酵２０分鐘後，分成每份６０公克之小麵糰，壓平，以擀麵棍擀開後，翻面，下端往兩旁稍拉開使其呈下寬上窄狀（圖１），再由上往下密實地捲成圓筒狀後，搓長並固定一端，另一端往同一方向旋轉（圖２），最後將兩端拉在一起（圖３）即成桔子麻花甜甜圈。
4. 鍋熱入油６杯燒至１５０℃，入桔子麻花甜甜圈以小火炸至兩面呈金黃色後，取出趁熱沾上細砂糖即可。

$5^{1}/_{3}$ oz. (150 g) .... oranges (net weight)
$2^{2}/_{3}$ oz. (75 g) ... shortening
$^{2}/_{3}$ oz. (18 g) ...... active dry yeast
as needed granulated sugar

1
- $3^{1}/_{2}$ oz. (100 g) ...... eggs
- $2^{2}/_{3}$ oz. (75 g) .... granulated sugar
- $^{2}/_{3}$ oz. (20 g) .... milk powder
- 1 t. .... salt

2
- $12^{1}/_{3}$ oz. (350 g). bread flour
- $5^{1}/_{3}$ oz. (150 g) ...... cake flour
- 1 t. ...... baking powder

1. Peel the oranges and discard all membranes; crush with a fork. Mix with **1**.
2. Dissolve the yeast with 3 T. water; mix with **1** mixture and sifted **2**. Add in shortening and mix well. This is the dough.
3. Let the dough rise at room temperature for 20 minutes. Divide into $2^{1}/_{6}$ oz. (60 g) small dough balls, then press each flat. Roll each piece out, turn upside down. Pull the lower two sides out to form a bell shape (illus. 1). Roll it up as a tight cylinder, and knead it into a long strip. Twist (illus. 2) and seal the two ends together (illus. 3).
4. Heat a frying pot, add 6 C. oil and heat to 150°C (300°F). Deep fry the twisters over low heat until golden on both sides. Dust on granulated sugar while still warm.

三味甜甜圈 · Doughnuts with Savory Fillings

發酵好之酵母甜甜圈麵糰 3份
麵包粉 .... 適量

咖哩餡：
絞肉 150公克
洋蔥丁 100公克
咖哩粉、麵粉 各2小匙
鹽 3/4小匙

鮪魚沙拉餡：
油漬鮪魚 120公克
洋蔥、沙拉醬 各60公克
黑胡椒粉 .... 少許

酸菜餡：
酸菜 300公克
糖 5大匙
味精、胡椒粉 各1/8小匙

1. 咖哩餡：鍋熱入油２大匙燒熱，入咖哩粉炒香，續入洋蔥丁拌炒，再入絞肉炒熟，加鹽、麵粉拌勻後，入水５大匙炒勻，分成８等份備用。
2. 鮪魚沙拉餡：油漬鮪魚壓碎，洋蔥切細丁，與沙拉醬、黑胡椒粉拌勻後，分成８等份備用。
3. 酸菜餡：
   （１）酸菜洗淨切碎，再以清水搓洗去除鹽份備用。
   （２）鍋熱入油２大匙燒熱，入酸菜、糖、味精、胡椒粉拌炒均勻後，分成８等份備用。
4. 將發酵好之酵母多拿滋麵糰分成２４等份，再擀成片狀（圖１），分別包入一份內餡（圖２），沾點水（圖３）並均勻沾上麵包粉後（圖４），繼續發酵３０分鐘即為三味多拿滋。
5. 鍋熱入油８杯燒至１２０℃，入三味多拿滋以小火炸至表面呈金黃色即可。

3 quantities raised doughnut dough
as needed bread crumbs

Curry filling:
5 1/3 oz.(150 g) ground pork
3 1/2 oz.(100 g) diced onion
2 t. each: curry powder, flour
3/4 t. .... salt

Tuna fish salad filling :
4 1/4 oz.(120 g) canned tuna fish
2 oz.(60 g) each: .... diced onion, mayonnaise
a dash of black pepper

Pickle filling:
10 2/3 oz. (300 g) .... sour mustard
5 T. .... sugar
1/8 t. .... pepper

1. Curry filling: Heat the wok, add 2 T oil; stir fry curry powder until fragrant. Add diced onion to fry, then add in pork. Stir fry until pork is done, season with salt. Add in flour and mix well, add 5 T. water and mix well. Divide into 8 equal portions.
2. Tuna fish salad filling: Mash tuna to smaller pieces. Mix tuna with onion, mayonnaise, and black pepper well. Divide into 8 equal portions.
3. Pickle filling:
   (1) Wash and chop sour mustard. Rinse under cold water to get rid off the salt.
   (2) Heat a wok, add 2 T. oil. Stir fry sour mustard, sugar, and pepper. Mix them well. Divide into 8 equal portions.
4. Divide raised doughnut dough into 24 equal portions. Roll them into flat pieces (illus. 1). Wrap a portion of filling in (illus. 2). Brush with a little water (illus. 3) and evenly dust with bread crumbs (illus. 4). Leave to rise for 30 minutes.
5. Heat the frying pot, add 8 C. oil and heat to 120 °C (250 °F). Deep fry the doughnuts over low heat until golden.

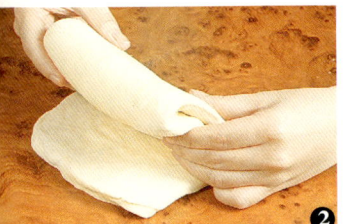

三角鬆餅 · Filled Pastry Deltas

起酥瑪琪琳	180 公克 (90%)
高筋麵粉	160 公克 (80%)
冰水	100 公克 (50%)
肉鬆	60 公克 (30%)
蛋液	60 公克 (30%)
低筋麵粉	40 公克 (20%)
白油	20 公克 (10%)
細砂糖	6 公克 (3%)

1 烤箱預熱至 220℃；高筋麵粉及低筋麵粉混合過篩；細砂糖入冰水溶解；肉鬆分成 6 等份備用。

2 麵粉置桌面上，中央挖空築成粉牆狀後，倒入糖水，由內往外輕輕拌勻成麵糊（圖 1），再入白油拌勻，入冰箱冷藏鬆弛 30 分鐘，取出包入起酥瑪琪琳，續入冰箱鬆弛 30 分鐘。

3 將麵糊擀成長方形薄片，再折三折（圖 2），入冰箱冷藏 10 分鐘，如此重覆三次，最後擀成 0.2 公分厚之方形片，以滾輪刀切成 10×10 公分之片狀 6 片，每片包入一份肉鬆，四週刷上蛋液，對折成三角形（圖 3）並輕按使其黏住，再以滾輪刀切去多餘部份，置於烤盤上，表面刷上蛋液後，入烤箱烤約 20 分鐘，關掉電源再續燜 10 分鐘，取出待涼即可。

6 1/3 oz. (180 g) .... sheet margarine(90%)
5 2/3 oz. (160 g) .... bread flour(80%)
2/5 C. .... ice water(50%)
2 oz. (60 g) .... seasoned pork fibers (30%)
2 oz. (60 g) .... beaten eggs(30%)
1 1/2 oz. (40 g) .... cake flour(20%)
2/3 oz. (20 g) .... shortening(10%)
1/5 oz. (6 g) ...... granulated sugar(3%)

1 Preheat oven to 220 °C (430 °F). Sift bread flour and cake flour. Dissolve the sugar in ice water. Divide the seasoned pork fibers into 6 equal portions.

2 Build a flour wall on a work table, pour the sugar water into the center hole. Work the flour from center outward, gently mix it into a dough (illus.1). Mix in the shortening. Rest in refrigerator for 30 minutes. Fold in sheet margarine. Again let it rest in refrigerator for 30 minutes.

3 Roll the dough into a rectangular sheet, fold it into three layers (illus. 2). Chill in refrigerator for 10 minutes. Repeat three times. Roll it into 0.2 cm (0.1 ") thin square sheet. With a pastry cutter, cut out 6 pieces of 10 cm X 10 cm (4 "x 4") squares. Wrap in a portion of pork fibers, brush the edges with beaten eggs; fold into triangles (illus. 3). Lightly press on the edges to seal. Trim off the excess with pastry cutter. Place on a baking sheet, brush the surfaces with beaten eggs. Bake in the oven for 20 minutes. Turn off the heat and let them stand in the oven for extra 10 minutes before removing. Allow to cool and serve.

鳳梨酥 · Chinese Pineapple Cakes

鳳梨餡	300 公克 (167%)
中筋麵粉	180 公克 (100%)
蛋黃	45 公克 (25%)
奶粉	13.5公克 (7.5%)

❶
- 酥油 .... 72 公克 (40%)
- 奶油 .... 54 公克 (30%)
- 糖粉 .... 36 公克 (20%)

1. 烤箱預熱至１６０℃；中筋麵粉過篩；鳳梨餡表面沾上少許麵粉使其不黏手，分成２０等份備用。
2. 將 ❶ 料打至顏色變淡後，入奶粉拌勻，再入蛋黃拌勻（分次慢慢加入），最後入中筋麵粉輕輕壓拌均勻（不可拌太久以免出筋），分成２０等份即為鳳梨酥皮。
3. 每份酥皮包上一份鳳梨餡後，搓成外表光滑之橢圓形（圖１），壓入模型內（圖２）再扣出（圖３），置於烤盤上，入烤箱烤１２分鐘，翻面續烤８分鐘即可。

■ 本配方成品極酥脆，碰觸較易碎裂，故可將配方內酥油及奶油量改為２０％。

- $10^{2}/_{3}$ oz. (300 g) . pineapple filling (167 %)
- $6^{1}/_{3}$ oz. (180 g) all purpose flour (100 %)
- $1^{2}/_{3}$ oz. (45 g) .... egg yolk (25 %)
- $1/2$ oz. (13.5 g) .... milk powder (7.5 %)

❶
- $2^{1}/_{2}$ oz. (72 g) ..... butter oil substitute (40 %)
- 2 oz. (54 g) butter (30 %)
- $1^{1}/_{4}$ oz. (36 g) powdered sugar (20 %)

1. Preheat oven to 160 °C (320 °F). Sift flour. Dust the pineapple filling with a little flour to prevent sticking to the fingers; divide into 20 equal portions.
2. Cream ❶ until light and fluffy, beat in milk powder, then mix in egg yolk (a little at a time). Fold in the flour and gently press on to mix (do not stir too long). Divide the dough into 20 equal portions.
3. Fill each with a portion of pineapple filling (illus. 1). Press into a mode (illus. 2) and invert onto a baking sheet (illus. 3). Bake in the oven for 12 minutes. Turn and bake the other side for another 8 minutes.

* The shells of pineapple cakes from this recipe are very crispy, easy to break if not handled carefully. The butter and butter oil substitute content may be reduced to 20 % for harder shells.

菊花酥 · Chrysanthemum Pastries

水油皮：
中筋麵粉 ...... 200 公克 (100%)
水 .... 84 公克 (42%)
豬油 .... 80 公克 (40%)
糖粉 .... 40 公克 (20%)
鹽 .... 1 公克 (0.5%)
油酥：
低筋麵粉 .... 132 公克 (66%)
豬油 .... 66 公克 (33%)

豆沙 .... 400 公克 (200%)
黑芝麻 .... 少許

1. 烤箱預熱至１８０℃備用。
2. 水油皮：中筋麵粉、糖粉、鹽混合過篩後，將中央挖空築成粉牆狀，倒入豬油、水，由內往外輕輕拌勻成麵糰，放置鬆弛１５－２０分鐘。
   油酥：低筋麵粉、豬油攪拌均勻即可。
3. 水油皮、油酥、豆沙均分成２０等份備用。
4. 每份水油皮包入一份油酥，接縫處朝上，稍壓後擀成薄片，捲成圓筒狀鬆弛１０分鐘，稍壓後再擀平，折三折（圖１），鬆弛１０分鐘，再稍壓擀成圓片狀，包入豆沙並擀成直徑８公分之圓形，周圍剪成１２瓣（圖２），將剪開之花瓣翻轉（圖３）使豆沙處朝上，置於烤盤中，表面刷上蛋黃液後（有豆沙處不要刷），中央再點上黑芝麻，入烤箱烤１３分鐘即可。

Water-shortening dough:
7 oz. (200 g) ... all purpose flour (100%)
1/3 C. .... water (42%)
3 oz. (80 g) lard or shortening (40%)
1 1/2 oz. (40 g) ..... powdered sugar (20%)
1/4 t. .... salt (0.5%)

Flaky dough:
4 2/3 oz. (132 g) .. cake flour (66%)
2 1/3 oz. (66 g) lard or shortening (33%)

14 1/3 oz. (400 g) .... red bean paste
as needed black sesame seeds

1. Preheat oven to 180 °C (355° F).
2. Water-shortening dough: Sift flour, sugar and salt together. Build a flour wall on a working table, pour lard or shortening and water into the center hole. Work the flour from center outward. Allow the dough to rest for 15 to 20 minutes. Flaky dough: Mix flour and lard or shortening well.
3. Divide each dough and red bean paste into 20 equal portions.
4. Wrap a portion of flaky dough inside each piece of water-shortening dough. Roll out to thin slices and then roll up into cylinders. Rest the dough for 10 minutes. Gently press to flatten, roll out until thin and fold into thirds (illus. 1). Rest for 10 minutes. Press slightly and roll into rounds. Wrap a portion of red bean paste in a piece of dough. Shape them into round flattened pieces. Snip with scissors to resemble chrysanthemum (illus. 2). Turn each petal outward (illus. 3), the red bean paste side should be facing up. Place on a baking sheet, brush the uncut center with beaten egg yolk and decorate with black sesame seeds. Bake for 13 minutes.

核桃酥 · Walnut Cookies

低筋麵粉	200 公克 (100%)
碎核桃	40 公克 (20%)

1
- 細砂糖 .... 120 公克 (60%)
- 酥油 .... 120 公克 (60%)
- 轉化糖漿 .... 10 公克 (5%)
- 泡打粉（過篩） .... 2 公克 (1%)
- 鹽 .... 1 公克 (0.5%)

2
- 蛋液 .... 10 公克 (5%)
- 水 .... 10 公克 (5%)
- 小蘇打 .... 2 公克 (1%)
- 氨粉 .... 2 公克 (1%)

1. 烤箱預熱至１７０℃備用。
2. **1**料置不銹鋼盆中，以打蛋器拌勻打至酥油顏色變淡（圖1）；**2**料拌勻，分二次倒入**1**料中打勻，再入碎核桃拌勻。
3. 麵粉過篩，中央挖空築成粉牆狀後（圖2），倒入作法2之材料輕輕拌勻即成麵糰（不可搓揉）。
4. 將麵糰分成每份４０公克之小麵糰，搓圓後置於烤盤上（每個麵糰中央用食指插一孔洞（圖3），以利烤焙時麵糰之擴張），入烤箱烤8分鐘，再關掉下火續烤5分鐘即可。

- 7 oz.(200 g) cake flour (100 %)
- 1 1/2 oz. (40 g) .... crushed walnuts (20%)

1
- 4 1/4 oz. (120 g) .... granulated sugar (60%)
- 4 1/4 oz. (120 g) butter oil substitute (60%)
- 1/3 oz. (10 g) invert syrup (5%)
- 1/2 t. sifted baking powder (1%)
- 1/4 t. salt (0.5%)

2
- 1/3 oz.(10 g) beaten egg (5%)
- 1/2 T. water (5%)
- 1/2 t. baking soda (1%)
- 1/2 t. Hartshorn salt (1%, maybe replaced by double quantity of baking powder)

1. Preheat oven to 170 ˚C (340 ˚F).
2. Cream **1** until light and fluffy (illus. 1). Mix **2**, pour half into **1** and mix well; then pour the other half in and mix well. Add walnuts.
3. Sift the flour, build a flour wall on a work table (illus. 2). Pour the ingredient **1**, **2** mixture into the center hole. Mix gently (do not knead).
4. Divide the dough into 1 1/3 oz. (40 g) small balls. Press a dent in the center with index finger to facilitate better dough rising (illus. 3). Bake in preheated oven for 8 minutes. Turn off the heat and leave them in the oven for extra 5 minutes before removing.

派皮製作 · Basic Pie Shell

| 中筋麵粉 .... 180公克 |
| 冰硬的奶油 .... 120公克 |
| 蛋黃 .... ½個 |

1
- 冰水 3大匙
- 細砂糖 .... ½大匙
- 鹽 .... ½小匙

1. 烤箱預熱至220℃；中筋麵粉過篩；奶油切丁；9寸圓形模型內塗奶油或白油備用（圖1）。
2. 奶油用麵刀邊切邊與中筋麵粉拌勻（圖2），再加 **1** 料，用壓的方式拌壓成糰（圖3）。
3. 麵糰兩面鋪上麵粉，用擀麵棍擀成比派盤大2寸的圓皮（圖4）。
4. 將圓皮鋪在派盤上，邊緣壓平，靜置鬆弛10分鐘後，用麵刀把周圍多出來的麵皮切掉即為派皮（圖5）。
5. 派皮用叉子刺洞（避免膨脹），並在邊緣壓出花紋後（圖6），入烤箱烤20分鐘，取出派皮，在邊緣處刷上蛋黃液，續入烤箱烤10分鐘即可。

---

6 oz. (180g) all purpose flour
4¼ oz. (120g) chilled butter or margarine
½ egg yolk

1
- 3 T. ice water
- ½ T. granulated sugar
- ½ t. salt

1. Preheat oven to 220°C (430 °F). Sift the flour. Dice the butter or margarine. Grease a 9" pie mold (illus. 1).
2. Cut the butter or margarine into sifted flour (illus. 2), add in **1** and knead into a dough (illus. 3).
3. Dust flour on both sides of the dough and roll out the dough to a pie sheet 2" larger than the pie mold (illus. 4).
4. Spread the pastry on the mold, press along the edges to fit into the mold. Leave to rest for 10 minutes. Trim off the excess edges (illus. 5).
5. Prick the shell with a fork to prevent raising, flute the edges (illus. 6). Bake for 20 minutes. Brush the edges with beaten egg yolk and bake for 10 minutes more.

波士頓派 · Boston Pie

低筋麵粉 .... 125 公克
香草精 .... 1 大匙
鮮奶油 .... 1 杯
糖粉 .... 3 大匙

❶ ┌ 細砂糖 .... 125 公克
   │ 蛋 .... 3 個
   └ 蛋黃 .... 2 個

1 烤箱預熱至１６０℃；低筋麵粉過篩。
2 ❶料打至鬆發後（體積約增為２至３倍），入香草精及低筋麵粉，用麵刀輕輕拌壓均勻後，倒入８寸烤盤，抹平表面，再入烤箱烤３０分鐘，取出待涼。
3 鮮奶油打發後，將烤好之派橫切成三片（底部稍厚）（圖１），底部置盤內，每個切面塗上鮮奶油疊起來（圖２），最後灑上過篩之糖粉即可（圖３）。

4 1/2 oz. (125g) cake flour
1 t. vanilla extract
4 C. whipped cream
3 T. powdered sugar

❶ ┌ 4 1/2 oz. (125g) granulated sugar
   │ 3 eggs
   └ 2 egg yolks

1 Preheat oven to 160 °C (320° F). Sift flour.
2 Beat ❶ until frothy (volume increases 2 to 3 times). Add vanilla extract and cake flour; use knife to cut in and gently knead evenly. Pour into a 8 " round baking tin. Level the top with a spatula. Bake for 30 minutes. Remove and leave to cool.
3 Slice the cake into three bases (the bottom one thickest) (illus. 1). Place the bottom layer on a cake plate, spread a layer of whipped topping on each base; then sandwich the bases together (illus. 2). Sprinkle powdered sugar over the top (illus. 3).

轉化糖漿
Invert Syrup

水 .... 1000公克(100%)　　細砂糖 500公克(50%)
蛋液 .... 20公克(20%)　　白醋　 15公克(15%)
酸梅 .... 3粒　　檸檬　 3片
鳳梨 3片

* 除蛋液外，全部材料均入不銹鋼鍋中以小火煮一小時後（煮時不可攪拌，但鍋邊一定要用刷子沾水刷乾淨，以免附著結晶體），再入蛋液，待蛋花浮起後過濾，濾汁以小火續煮半小時，最後倒入乾淨玻璃瓶內待涼，蓋上蓋子放置一週即可使用。

4 1/5 C. water (100%)
1 1/6 lb. (500 g) castor sugar (50%)
2/3 oz. (20 g) beaten egg (20%)
1/2 oz. (15 g) white vinegar (15%)
3 preserved prunes
3 slices lemon
3 slices pineapple

* Put all ingredients, except the beaten egg, into a stainless pot and simmer over low heat for one hour (do not stir during simmering). Clean the sides with a wet brush to prevent accumulating crystallized sediments. Turn off the heat and add in beaten egg (do not stir). As soon as the egg floats on the top, sieve through a colander. Simmer the clean syrup again over low heat for half an hour. Pour into a clean, dry glass jar and allow to cool. Cover with lid and let stand for one week. Then it is ready to use.

鹼水
Lye

水 .... 100公克(100%)
鹼粉 .... 25公克(25%)
小蘇打 .... 1公克(1%)

* 全部材料入鍋煮化待涼即可（不可攪拌）。

1/2 C. water (100%)
1 oz. (25 g) powdered lye (25%)
1/4 t. baking soda

* Bring all ingredients to a boil and allow to cool (do not stir).

鹼水 Lye

轉化糖漿 Invert Syrup

塔皮製作 Basic Tart Shell Dough

蛋塔
Custard Tarts

塔皮麵糰	1份（12個）	水	125公克
奶水	100公克	細砂糖	60公克
蘭姆酒	1/8小匙	蛋	2個

1 烤箱預熱至２００℃備用。
2 水與細砂糖拌勻至糖溶化，入奶水、蛋及蘭姆酒拌勻，再過篩即成蛋塔餡。
3 塔皮麵糰分成１２等份,每份塔皮均勻壓入塔模後,將蛋塔餡填入塔模內約八分滿,再入烤箱烤２５分鐘即可。

1 quantity basic tart shell dough
$^1/_2$ C. water
$^2/_5$ C. evaporated milk
$2^1/_4$ oz. (60 g) granulated sugar
$^1/_8$ t. rum
2 eggs

1 Preheat oven to 200° C (390° F).
2 Mix water and sugar until sugar dissolves. Add evaporated milk, eggs and rum. Sieve the mixture through a colander.
3 Divide the tart dough into 12 small tart shells, press into tart molds. Fill the tarts with the egg mixture. Bake in the oven for 25 minutes.

塔皮製作
Basic Tart Shell Dough

低筋麵粉	170公克	奶油	50公克
糖粉	50公克	奶粉	50公克
蛋	1個		

1 低筋麵粉過篩，奶油切小丁（圖１）置室溫下軟化備用。
2 取一鋼盆入奶油及糖粉打至奶油顏色變淡（圖２），再入奶粉及蛋攪拌均勻（圖３），最後入低筋麵粉輕輕拌壓均勻即成塔皮麵糰（圖４）（輕拌即可，以避免出筋使塔皮失去脆度）。
3 將塔皮麵糰分成每份３０公克之小麵糰１２份（圖５），取塔模將塔皮麵糰壓入模型內即可（圖６）。

6 oz. (170 g) cake flour
$1^2/_3$ oz. (50 g) butter or margarine
$1^2/_3$ oz. (50 g) powdered sugar
$1^2/_3$ oz. (50 g) milk powder
1 egg

1 Sift flour. Dice butter or margarine (illus. 1) and allow to soften at room temperature.
2 Cream butter or margarine and sugar until light and fluffy (illus. 2). Add milk powder and egg; mix well (illus. 3). Gently knead in flour (illus. 4)(do not over-knead, or the crust will not be crispy).
3 Divide the dough into 12 small balls (about 30 g or 1 oz. each) (illus. 5). Press the dough balls into tart molds (illus. 6).

蛋塔 Custard Tarts

加拿許塔 Canache Pie

黑櫻桃杏仁塔
Black Cherry Tarts

塔皮麵糰	1份	黑櫻桃（罐頭）	12顆
蛋	130公克	杏仁霜	100公克
低筋麵粉	20公克	果醬	1大匙

1｛奶油 100公克
　　細砂糖 80公克

1 烤箱預熱至200℃；低筋麵粉過篩；每顆黑櫻桃切成4等份備用。
2 塔皮麵糰分成12等份，每份塔皮均勻壓入塔模中備用。
3 **1**料打發至奶油顏色變淡，入蛋拌勻，再入杏仁霜、低筋麵粉拌勻後，裝入擠花袋內，擠入塔模中約八分滿，再用黑櫻桃裝飾，入烤箱烤15分鐘後取出，表面再塗上果醬即可。

1 quantity basic tart shell dough
12 canned dark cherries
4 1/2 oz. (130 g) eggs
3 1/2 oz. (100 g) ground almonds
2/3 oz. (20 g) cake flour
1 T. jam

1｛ 3 1/2 oz. (100 g) butter or margarine
　　2 3/4 oz. (80 g) granulated sugar

1 Preheat oven to 200° C (390° F). Sift flour. Cut each cherry into quarters.
2 Divide tart shell dough into 12 tart shells, press into tart molds.
3 Cream **1** until light and fluffy, beat in the eggs and mix well. Add ground almonds, flour and mix. Place the filling into a piping bag, pipe into the shells, about 80 % full. Decorate the top with cherries. Bake for 15 minutes. Remove. Spread jam over the top.

加拿許塔
Canache Pie

| 塔皮麵糰 | 1份 | 奶油蘇打小西餅 | 120公克 |
| 巧克力米 | 50公克 | | |

1｛巧克力 250公克
　　鮮奶油 60公克
　　奶水 60公克

1 烤箱預熱至180℃；塔皮麵糰分成12等份，每份塔皮均勻壓入塔模後，入烤箱烤25分鐘，取出待涼備用。
2 **1**料入鍋煮溶化，待涼，續入壓碎之奶油蘇打小西餅拌勻即成加拿許。
3 取一塔皮，填入加拿許後，再灑上巧克力米即可。

1 quantity basic tart shell dough
4 1/4 oz. (120 g) cream soda cracker
1 2/3 oz. (50 g) chocolate rice

1｛ 9 oz. (250 g) chocolate
　　2 1/4 oz. (60 g) fresh cream
　　4 T. evaporated milk

1 Preheat oven to 180 °C (355 °F). Divide the dough into 12 tart shells, press into tart molds. Bake for 25 minutes. Remove and leave them to cool.
2 Melt **1** in a double boiler, leave to cool. Add into crushed crackers and mix well. This is the canache filling.
3 Fill the tart shells with canache filling and sprinkle on chocolate rice.

黑櫻桃杏仁塔 Black Cherry Tarts

杏仁塔 · Almond Tarts

- 塔皮麵糰 1份
- 杏仁片 50公克
- 蛋 1個
- ①
  - 細砂糖 80公克
  - 酥油 60公克
- ②
  - 起司粉 2小匙
  - 低筋麵粉 45公克
  - 泡打粉 1/2小匙
- ③
  - 核桃 30公克
  - 葡萄乾 20公克

1. 烤箱預熱至200℃；低筋麵粉過篩，核桃入烤箱烤5分鐘後，取出切碎。
2. 塔皮麵糰分成12等份（圖1），每份塔皮均勻壓入塔模中（圖2）。
3. ❶料打發至酥油顏色變淡（圖3），再入蛋、❷料拌勻，最後入❸料混合均勻即為餡。
4. 取一塔皮，填入餡料約七分滿，表面再撒上杏仁片後，入烤箱烤20分鐘即可。

- 1 .... quantity basic tart shell dough
- 1 2/3 oz. (50 g) .... almond slices
- 1 .... egg
- ❶
  - 2 3/4 oz. (80 g) granulated sugar
  - 2 1/4 oz. (60 g) ..... butter oil substitute
- ❷
  - 1 1/2 oz. (45 g) cake flour
  - 2 t. ... grated Parmesan cheese
  - 1/2 t. .... baking powder
- ❸
  - 1 oz. ..... (30 g) walnuts
  - 2/3 oz. ..... (20 g) raisins

1. Preheat oven to 200° C (390° F). Sift flour. Roast walnuts for 5 minutes, and chop.
2. Divide the tart shell dough into 12 tart shells, press into tart molds.
3. Cream ❶ until light and fluffy, beat in egg and ❷. Add ❸ and mix well to be the filling.
4. Fill the tarts with filling, about 70 % full. Sprinkle the top with almond slices. Bake for 20 minutes.

核桃塔 · Walnut Tarts

塔皮麵糰	1份
核桃	90公克
杏仁片	30公克

1
- 細砂糖 …… 70公克
- 奶水 …… 25公克
- 葡萄乾 …… 20公克
- 蘭姆酒 …… 1/2 小匙
- 蛋 …… 1/2 個

2
- 蛋黃 …… 6個
- 細砂糖 …… 30公克
- 泡打粉 …… 1/4 小匙
- 蛋 …… 1/2 個

1 杏仁片、核桃先入160℃烤箱烤熟後切碎（圖1），與**1**料拌勻即成餡。
2 塔皮麵糰分成12等份，每份塔皮均勻壓入塔模後（圖2），填入內餡備用。
3 **2**料用打蛋器打至濃稠狀（圖3），放入平口擠花袋中，擠在餡上，再入180℃烤箱烤30分鐘即可。

---

1 ……… quantity basic tart shell dough
3 1/4 oz. (90 g) …….. walnuts
1 oz. (30 g) . almond slices

1
- 2 1/3 oz. (70 g) …………… granulated sugar
- 1 2/3 T. evaporated milk
- 2/3 oz. (20 g) …… raisins
- 1/2 t. rum
- 1/2 egg

2
- 6 egg yolks
- 1 oz. (30 g) granulated sugar
- 1/4 t. …. baking powder
- 1/2 egg

1 Roast almond slices and walnuts in a preheated oven of 160 °C (320 °F) until done; chop into small pieces (illus. 1). Mix the nuts with **1** to become the filling.
2 Divide the dough into 12 tart shells (illus. 2). Fill with nut mixture.
3 Beat **2** with a mixer until thicken (illus. 3). Place into a piping bag and pipe on top of filling. Bake in a preheated oven of 180 °C (355° F) for 30 minutes.

草莓戚風派 · Strawberry Chiffon Pie

烤好派皮（9寸）	1 份
罐頭草莓	200 公克
蛋	130 公克
細砂糖	10 公克
檸檬汁	1 大匙
鮮奶油	1/2 杯
❶ 水	1/4 杯
吉利丁	1 1/2 大匙
蘭姆酒	1 大匙

1. 草莓 取 6 顆切對半備用，其餘加檸檬汁用果汁機打成泥狀。
2. ❶料調勻入鍋隔水加熱至吉利丁完全溶化（圖 1）。
3. 蛋黃、蛋白分開，將蛋白打至起泡後，入糖打至硬性發泡（圖 2）。蛋黃加 ❶料及草莓泥拌勻，再入發泡蛋白拌勻，最後倒入烤好之派皮中抹平，置冰箱冷藏凝結。
4. 鮮奶油打發,用擠花袋擠在草莓派上後，排上草莓（圖 3）即可。

1 (9")	baked pie shell
7 oz. (200 g)	canned strawberries
4 2/3 oz. (130 g)	eggs
1/3 oz. (10 g)	granulated sugar
1 T.	lemon juice
2 C.	whipped cream
❶ 1/4 C.	water
1 1/2 T.	gelatin
1 T.	rum

1. Cut 6 strawberries to halves. Puree the rest of strawberries with lemon juice in a juicer.
2. Mix ❶ and melt in a double boiler until gelatin dissolves (illus. 1).
3. Separate the egg yolks and egg whites. Beat the egg whites until frothy, add sugar and beat until stiff peaks form (illus. 2). Mix egg yolks with strawberry puree; fold into egg whites. Pour into pie shell, even the top with a spatula. Chill in refrigerator until set.
4. Pipe whipped topping on the strawberry pie. Decorate the top with halved strawberries (illus. 3).

巧克力戚風派 · Chocolate Chiffon Pie

烤好派皮（9寸）	1份
細砂糖	40公克
巧克力醬	40公克
蛋	2個
鮮奶油	1杯
❶ 巧克力	100公克
牛奶	1/2杯
吉利丁	1大匙

1. 蛋白、蛋黃分開備用。
2. ❶料入鍋隔水加熱至巧克力溶化（圖1），再入蛋黃拌勻即成巧克力蛋黃汁。
3. 蛋白用打蛋器打至起泡後，加糖打至硬性發泡（圖2），再入巧克力蛋黃汁拌勻，倒入派皮中，抹平表面，置冰箱冷藏凝結即為巧克力派。
4. 取出巧克力派，淋上巧克力醬後，將鮮奶油打發，用擠花袋擠在派上即可（圖3）。

- 1 (9") .... baked pie shell
- 1 1/3 oz. (40 g) ... granulated sugar
- 1 1/3 oz. (40 g) ..... chocolate fudge
- 2 .... eggs
- 4 C. .... whipped cream
- ❶ 3 1/2 oz. (100 g) .... chocolate
- 　1/2 C. .... milk
- 　1 T. .... gelatin

1. Separate egg yolks and egg whites.
2. Place ❶ in a double boiler and heat until chocolate melts (illus. 1). Add egg yolks and mix well.
3. Beat the egg whites until frothy, add the sugar and continue to beat until stiff peaks form (illus. 2). Pour in egg yolk mixture and mix well. Pour it into the pie shell, level the top with a spatula. Chill in refrigerator until set.
4. Frost the pie with chocolate fudge and decorate with whipped topping (illus. 3).

鮮肉小派餃 · Petite Pork Pies

派皮麵糊 .... 2 份
絞肉 .... 250 公克
蛋黃 .... 1 個

1 蔥末、薑末、洋蔥末 .... 各35 公克
   酒、麻油 .... 各1 大匙
   鹽 .... 3/4 小匙
   味精、胡椒粉 各 1/4 小匙

1 烤箱預熱至２００℃；絞肉用刀再剁細，入鋼盆與**1**料拌勻、摔打至有彈性即為肉餡，分成１２等份備用。
2 將派皮麵糊入冰箱冷凍１０分鐘，取出擀成大張薄片（約０‧３公分厚）（圖１），再用滾輪刀切成１０公分平方之麵皮１２份（圖２）。
3 取一麵皮塗上蛋黃液後，填入一份肉餡，以對角方式對折壓緊成三角形（圖３），置於烤盤上，表面再塗上蛋黃液，用牙籤均勻刺洞後，入烤箱烤３０分鐘至表面呈金黃色即可。

2 .... quantities basic pie shell dough
9 oz. (250 g) ground pork
1 .... egg yolk

1 1 1/4 oz. (35g) each: minced green onion, minced ginger, minced onion
   1 T. each: rice wine, sesame oil
   3/4 t. .... salt
   1/4 t. .... pepper

1 Preheat oven to 200 °C (390° F).
2 Chop ground pork again with a knife, mix well with **1**; throw the mixture against a worktop to increase its texture. Divide into 12 equal portions.
3 Freeze the pie shell dough for 10 minutes, roll it out to a larger sheet (about 0.3 cm thick) (illus. 1). Cut the sheet into 12 pieces of 10 cm (4") squares with a pastry cutter (illus. 2).
4 Brush each piece of dough with beaten egg yolk, place a portion of pork filling inside. Fold one corner to the other corner; forming a triangle (illus. 3). Place the pies on a baking sheet, brush the surfaces again with beaten egg yolk; prick the top with a toothpick. Bake in a oven for 30 minutes or until golden.

廣式月餅 · Cantonese Moon Cakes

豆沙	300 公克
鹹蛋黃	12 個
高筋麵粉	1/4 杯
月餅模子(1.5兩)	1 個
蛋	1 個
米酒	1 大匙
低筋麵粉	70 公克(100%)
轉化糖漿	49公克(70%)
花生油	19 公克(28%)
鹼水	1/2 小匙(3%)

1. 烤箱預熱至２００℃；低筋麵粉過篩，中央挖空築成粉牆狀；豆沙分１２等份備用。
2. 鹹蛋黃洗淨，灑上米酒入烤箱烤熟後（約８分鐘），取出待涼。
3. 轉化糖漿、花生油、鹼水入鋼盆拌勻，倒入粉牆中與低筋麵粉慢慢壓拌均勻（圖１），鬆弛３０分鐘後，分成１２等份即為月餅皮。
4. 手沾少許低筋麵粉，將月餅皮壓扁，上置豆沙、蛋黃後輕輕收口（圖２）。月餅模子灑上少許高筋麵粉後倒扣出來，使麵粉均勻於模型上，再將包好之月餅均勻壓入模型內，左右敲兩下，最後從中間大力敲一下（圖３），使月餅脫出模型。
5. 月餅置烤盤上，入烤箱烤５分鐘，取出待涼，於表面刷兩次蛋液後，續烤５分鐘至表面呈金黃色即可。

10 1/2 oz. (300 g)	sweet red bean paste
12	yolks of salt-preserved eggs
1 T.	rice wine
1/4 C.	bread flour
1	moon cake mold (2 oz.)
1	egg
2 1/2 oz. (70 g)	cake flour (100%)
1 3/4 oz.(49 g)	invert syrup (70%)
2/3 oz. (19 g)	peanut oil (28%)
1/2 t.	lye

1. Preheat oven to 200°C (390°F). Sift cake flour, build a flour wall on a working table. Divide the red bean paste into 12 equal portions.
2. Rinse salted egg yolks, sprinkle on rice wine; bake in the oven until done (about 8 minutes). Remove and leave to cool.
3. Mix syrup, oil, and lye; pour into the center hole of the flour wall. Gently knead into a dough (illus. 1). Let it rest for 30 minutes, then divide the dough into 12 equal portions.
4. Dust some cake flour on the hands, flatten each piece of dough; wrap a portion of egg yolk and red bean paste inside, gently seal the openings (illus. 2). Dust some bread flour into the moon cake mold, invert and remove excess flour. Press a cake evenly into the mold, invert and knock once on each side, then pound once in the center (illus. 3), the cake will drop out of the mold.
5. Place the cake on a baking sheet, bake for 5 minutes. Remove and leave to cool. Brush the surfaces with beaten egg twice and bake again for 5 minutes or until golden.

蛋黃酥 · Oriental Surprises

豆沙	300 公克
鹹蛋黃	20 個
米酒	1 大匙
蛋	1 個
黑芝麻	1 大匙

1
- 中筋麵粉 ... 185 公克(100%)
- 水 ... 78 公克(42%)
- 豬油 ... 56 公克(30%)
- 糖粉 ... 37 公克(20%)

2
- 低筋麵粉 ... 140 公克(100%)
- 豬油 ... 70 公克(50%)

1. 烤箱預熱至１８０℃，中筋、低筋麵粉分別過篩備用。
2. 鹹蛋黃洗淨，灑上米酒入烤箱烤熟後（約８分鐘），取出待涼。
3. 豆沙分成２０等份，每份包入鹹蛋黃即為豆沙蛋黃餡。
4. **1**料拌勻成糊，以塑膠袋蓋住，放置鬆弛２０分鐘後，分２０等份；**2**料壓拌均勻亦分２０等份，再取**1**料包**2**料（圖１），擀薄後（圖２）捲起來，再擀開捲起，最後擀成圓形，包入蛋黃豆沙餡收口（圖３）。
5. 將蛋黃酥置烤盤上，入烤箱烤１０分鐘，取出，於表面刷兩次蛋液並灑上芝麻後，續烤１０分鐘至表面呈金黃色即可。

10½ oz. (300 g)	sweet red bean paste
20	yolks of salt-preserved eggs
1 T.	rice wine
1	egg
1 T.	black sesame seeds

1
- 6½ oz. (185 g) .... all purpose flour (100%)
- ⅓ C. .... water (42%)
- 2 oz. (56 g) ...... lard or shortening (30%)
- 1⅓ oz. (37 g) .... powdered sugar (20%)

2
- 5 oz. (140 g) .... cake flour (100%)
- 2½ oz. (70 g) ... lard or shortening (50%)

1. Preheat oven to 180°C (355°F). Sift all purpose flour, cake flour.
2. Rinse the salted egg yolks, sprinkle on rice wine and bake in the oven until done (about 8 minutes). Remove and leave to cool.
3. Divide the red bean paste into 20 equal portions, wrap an egg yolk in each.
4. Mix **1** into a dough, cover with plastic wrap and leave to rest for 20 minutes; then divide the dough into 20 equal portions. Mix **2** into a dough, divide the dough into 20 equal portions. Wrap each portion of **2** dough inside of each **1** dough (illus. 1). Roll out each piece of dough, then fold into thirds to form three layers (illus. 2). Roll out again and one more fold into thirds to form three layers. Then roll each portion into a small round (illus. 3). Wrap one portion of egg yolk-red bean paste inside, close the openings.
5. Bake in the oven for 10 minutes. Remove and brush the top with beaten egg yolk twice. Sprinkle on sesame seeds over the top. Bake again for 10 minutes or until golden.

蛋白打發程度 · Guide to whisk egg whites

濕性發泡
Soft peak form :

蛋白經攪拌後漸漸凝固起來，表面不規則的氣泡消失，而變為許多均勻的細小氣泡，蛋白潔白而具光澤，勾起時可成一細長尖峰而不垂彎。

Whisk the egg whites until the foam retains its shape. The irregular air bubbles on the surface will disappear and be replaced by soft peaks which remain on the whisk.

乾性發泡
Stiff peak form

蛋白繼續攪拌，此時無法看出氣泡的組織，顏色雪白而無光澤，用手指勾起時呈堅硬的尖鋒，即使將此尖鋒倒置也不會彎曲。

Continue to whisk until air bubbles no longer can be seen. The color remains snow white, but no longer shiny. The peaks are stiff and unbending when stirred up with a whisk.

棉花狀態
Cotton form

蛋白已完全成球形凝固狀，用手指無法勾起尖鋒。
The egg whites are whisked to form balls, no longer able to form any peaks.

奶油霜
Butter Cream

奶油 750公克	白油 750公克
糖粉 750公克	蘭姆酒 1大匙
沙拉油 .... 少許	

將糖粉、奶油、白油打發後，續入沙拉油拌打均勻（約2至3分鐘），最後加1大匙蘭姆酒拌勻即可。

1²⁄₃ lb. (750 g) butter
1²⁄₃ lb. (750 g) shortening
1²⁄₃ lb. (750 g) powdered sugar
1T. rum
as needed salad oil

Mix sugar, milk and shortening; beat until fluffy. Add in oil and mix well (about 2-3 minutes). Then, add in 1T. rum and mix well.

小蛋糕 Cup Cakes

海綿蛋糕
Sponge Cake

蛋液	222.5 公克 (48.33%)	低筋麵粉	150 公克(100%)
細砂糖	94 公克 (62.66%)	蜂蜜	44 公克 (29.33%)
奶油	32 公克 (21.33%)	奶水	30 公克(20%)
ester sp	20 公克 (13.33%)		

1. 烤箱預熱至１８０℃；１２×８．５公分之模型內塗油並撒上一層薄麵粉備用。
2. 蛋液與細砂糖攪拌均勻，入過篩之麵粉拌勻，再入 ester sp 打至乳白色後，加蜂蜜以慢速攪打５分鐘，最後入奶水及軟化之奶油輕輕拌勻即為麵糊。
3. 將麵糊倒入模型內，入烤箱中層烤１０分鐘後，移至上層續烤１０分鐘，取出待涼即可。
■ 烤箱溫度若有上、下火，將烤箱預熱至 上火１８０℃下火 １４０℃烤１０分鐘後，關掉上火續烤１０分鐘即可。

8 oz. (222.5 g) beaten eggs (148.33%)
$5^{1}/_{3}$ oz. (150 g) cake flour (100%)
$3^{1}/_{3}$ oz. (94 g) granulated sugar (62.66%)
$1^{1}/_{2}$ oz. (44 g) honey (29.33%)
1 oz.(32 g) butter or margarine (21.33%)
2 T. evaporated milk (20%)
$^{2}/_{3}$ oz. (20 g) ester sp (13.33%)

1. Preheat oven to 180°C (355°F). Grease and flour a 12 x 8.5 cm (5" x 3 $^{1}/_{2}$") baking mold.
2. Mix beaten eggs with granulated sugar, add sifted flour and mix well. Beat in ester sp until color turns to white. Add honey and beat for 5 minutes at low speed. Gently mix in milk and soft butter or margarine.
3. Pour the batter into the mold, bake at the center of oven for 10 minutes. Then on the upper rack of oven for 10 minutes. Remove and leave to cool.

小蛋糕
Cup Cakes

| 奶油 | 100 公克 | 低筋麵粉 | 85 公克 |
| 奶水 | 35 公克 | | |

1
- 蛋（淨重）．．．．．．．．75 公克
- 蛋黃．．．．．．．．．．．．75 公克
- 細砂糖．．．．．．．．．．75 公克

1. 烤箱預熱至１５０℃；低筋麵粉過篩；奶油置室溫下溶化備用。
2. **1** 料打發後，續打至糊狀，入奶水拌勻，再用麵刀將麵粉輕輕拌入，最後入奶油拌勻即成麵糊。
3. 將麵糊裝入擠花袋中，擠入墊有杯模紙之小布丁杯內，入烤箱中層烤約１０分鐘即可。
■ 烤箱溫度若有上、下火，則將烤箱預熱至上火２１０℃、下火１００℃

$3^{1}/_{2}$ oz. (100 g) butter or margarine
3 oz. (85 g) cake flour
$2^{1}/_{3}$ T. evaporated milk

1 $2^{2}/_{3}$ oz. (75 g) each: eggs (net weight), egg yolks, granulated sugar

1. Preheat oven to 150°C (300°F). Sift flour. Soften butter or margarine at room temperature.
2. Beat **1** until fluffy and smooth, beat in milk. Gently fold in the flour, add butter or margarine; mix well.
3. Pour the batter into a piping bag. Pipe into lined cup cake molds. Bake on the upper rack of the oven for 10 minutes.

海綿蛋糕 Sponge Cake

香草天使蛋糕 Vanilla Angel Cake

奶油蛋糕
Butter Cake

低筋麵粉	120公克	奶油	100公克
細砂糖	90公克	葡萄乾	70公克
蛋	3個	泡打粉	1/3 小匙

1. 烤箱預熱175℃；9.5 x 6.5 x18.5公分之方形模型內塗奶油並鋪上蛋糕紙備用。
2. 奶油置室溫下軟化，放入鋼盆中打勻，再入細砂糖打發至乳白色，續入打勻之蛋液（分次放入）攪拌均勻，最後入剁碎葡萄乾及過篩之麵粉、泡打粉拌勻即為麵糊。
3. 將麵糊倒入模型內，入烤箱中層烤25分鐘即可。

■ 烤箱溫度若有上、下火，則將烤箱預熱至上火200℃、下火150℃烤25分鐘即可。

4 1/4 oz. (120 g) cake flour
3 1/2 oz. (100 g) butter or margarine
3 1/4 oz. (90 g) granulated sugar
2 1/3 oz. (70 g) raisins
3 eggs
1/3 t. baking powder

1. Preheat oven to 175 °C (350°F). Grease and line a 9.5 x 18.5 x 6.5cm (4" x 7" x 2 3/4") square baking pan.
2. Soften the butter or margarine at room temperature, cream with a beater. Add granulated sugar and beat until light and fluffy. Mix in beaten eggs a little at a time. Then add chopped raisins, sifted flour and baking powder. Blend thoroughly.
3. Pour the batter into the baking pan. Bake at the center of the oven for 25 minutes.

香草天使蛋糕
Vanilla Angel Cake

| 蛋白 | 250公克(53.2%) | 細砂糖 | 145公克(30.9%) |
| 塔塔粉 | 3公克(0.6%) | 鹽 | 1.5公克(0.3%) |

① [低筋麵粉 ... 70公克(15%)
    香草精 .... 1 1/2 小匙]

1. 烤箱預熱至160℃；低筋麵粉混合過篩備用。
2. 蛋白與塔塔粉打發後，入細砂糖及鹽打至濕性發泡，再入 ① 料輕輕拌勻，倒入8吋空心圓模內，入烤箱中層烤10分鐘後，移至下層續烤10分鐘，取出倒扣待涼，再用鮮奶油裝飾表面即可。

■ 烤箱溫度若有上、下火，則將烤箱預熱至180℃、下火100℃即可。

9 oz. (250 g) egg whites (53.2%)
5 1/4 oz. (145 g) granulated sugar (30.9%)
3/4 t. cream of tartar(0.6%)
1/4 t. salt (0.3%)

① [2 1/2 oz. (70 g) cake flour (15%)
    1 1/2 t. vanilla extract]

1. Preheat oven to 160°C (320°F). Sift flour.
2. Whisk egg whites and cream of tartar until frothy; add granulated sugar and salt; beat until soft peaks form. Fold in ①, pour into a 8" savarin baking mold. Bake in the center of the oven for 10 minutes. Move the cake to the lower rack in the oven and bake for 10 minutes more. Remove from the oven, invert and leave to cool. Frost with whipped cream.

奶油蛋糕 Butter Cake

乳酪蛋糕 · Processed Cheddar Cheese Cake

乳酪（起司片）	285 公克
鮮奶油	145 公克
細砂糖	75 公克
低筋麵粉	37 公克
玉米粉	25 公克
蛋	4 個

1. 烤箱預熱至１８０℃；直徑２１．５公分之圓形模型內鋪上蛋糕紙；蛋黃與蛋白分開備用。
2. 乳酪、鮮奶油隔水加熱至溶化，待涼後，入過篩之低筋麵粉及玉米粉拌勻，再入蛋黃拌勻備用。
3. 蛋白打至起泡，入細砂糖續打至濕性發泡後，再入作法２之材料拌勻，倒入模型內，置於加水之烤盤中，入烤箱中層烤約２５分鐘後，將烤盤調頭，以１２０℃續烤６分鐘，最後於蛋糕上蓋紙，以１８０℃烤５分鐘即可。

■ 烤箱溫度若有上下火，則將烤箱預熱至上火１７０℃、下火１２０℃烤３０分鐘即可。

---

10 oz. (285 g) ...... cheddar cheese
5 1/4 oz. (145 g) .... fresh cream
2 2/3 oz. (75 g) ... granulated sugar
1 1/3 oz. (37 g) .... cake flour
1 oz. (25 g) .... corn flour
4 .... eggs

1. Preheat oven to 180°C (355°F). Line a 21.5 cm (10")round baking pan. Separate the eggs.
2. Heat cheddar cheese and fresh cream over water until dissolved, leave to cool. Stir together sifted cake flour, corn flour and cream mixture until smooth. Then add the egg yolks and mix well.
3. Whisk the egg whites until frothy, add granulated sugar and whisk until soft peak forms. Fold the egg whites into the flour mixture. Pour the batter into the baking pan. Place the baking pan in a water bath and bake at the center rack of oven for 25 minutes. Turn the direction to the other side, and bake at 120°C (250°F) for 6 minutes. Cover the cake with foil paper and bake for 5 more minutes. Remove.

菠蘿蛋糕 · Pineapple Cake

奶油	....	250 公克
低筋麵粉	....	250 公克
泡打粉	....	2 小匙
鳳梨汁	....	50 公克

1 ┌ 鳳梨片 .... 9 片
　　└ 細砂糖 .... 188 公克

2 ┌ 蛋 .... 6 個
　　└ 細砂糖 .... 200 公克

1. 烤箱預熱至１７０℃；**1**料以慢火煮至鳳梨片呈黏稠金黃色後（圖１），撈起待涼；２３×２５公分之方形烤盤舖上蛋糕紙，將煮好之鳳梨片平舖於上（圖２）；另取奶油加熱至５０℃時，離火備用。
2. **2**料打至鬆發為原來２倍量之蛋糊後，續入鳳梨汁拌勻，再入過篩之低筋麵粉、泡打粉及奶油輕輕攪拌均勻即成麵糊。
3. 將麵糊倒入舖有鳳梨片之烤盤中（圖３），入烤箱烤３５分鐘即可。

9 oz. (250 g) butter or margarine
9 oz. (250 g) ..... cake flour
2 t. .... baking powder
3 1/3 T. .... pineapple juice

1 ┌ 9 .... slices pineapple
　　│ 6 2/3 oz. (188 g) ....
　　└ granulated sugar

2 ┌ 6 eggs
　　│ 7 oz. (200 g) granulated
　　└ sugar

1. Preheat oven to 170°C (340°F). Cook **1** over low heat until pineapple slices turn to sticky golden (illus. 1). Remove pineapples and leave to cool. Arrange a layer of pineapple on a 23 x 25cm (8"x10") lined baking pan (illus. 2). Heat butter or margarine to 50°C (120°F), remove from heat.
2. Beat **2** until increasing to twice the volume, add pineapple juice. Blend in sifted flour, baking powder, and melted butter or margarine, mix gently until well blended.
3. Pour the batter over the pineapple slices in the baking pan (illus. 3). Bake for 35 minutes.

美式輕鬆草莓蛋糕 · American Strawberry Cake

沙拉油 .... 55 公克
草莓果醬 .... 1 罐

1
- 蛋白 .... 4 個
- 塔塔粉 .... ½ 小匙

2
- 細砂糖 .... 100 公克
- 蛋黃 .... 4 個
- 鹽 .... ⅕ 小匙

3
- 新鮮草莓汁 .... 40 公克
- 草莓粒 .... 4 粒

4
- 低筋麵粉 .... 70 公克
- 泡打粉 .... 8 公克

1. 烤箱預熱至１５０℃（３００°F）；**1** 料打至濕性發泡；**3** 料用果汁機打勻；**4** 料過篩備用。
2. **2** 料攪拌至糖溶化後，入沙拉油、**3** 料及 **4** 料拌勻，再入 **1** 料混和均勻即為麵糊。
3. 將麵糊倒入鋪有蛋糕紙之２３×２５公分方形烤盤中（圖１），入烤箱烤約２５分鐘後，取出待涼備用。
4. 取蛋糕一切為二（圖２），中間塗上果醬當夾層即可（圖３）。

■ 美式輕鬆橘子蛋糕：將美式輕鬆草莓蛋糕之 **3** 料改成柳橙濃縮汁４０公克，果醬改為橘子果醬，其餘作法均相同。

■ 美式輕鬆巧克力蛋糕：將美式輕鬆草莓蛋糕之 **3** 料改為巧克力醬４０公克，果醬夾層改為奶油霜即可。

2 oz. (55 g) vegetable oil
1 small jar strawberry jam

1
- 4 egg whites
- ½ t. cream of tartar

2
- 3½ oz. (100 g) granulated sugar
- 4 egg yolks
- ¼ t. salt

3
- 2⅔ T. fresh strawberry juice
- 4 strawberries

4
- 2½ oz. (70 g) cake flour
- ¼ oz. (8 g) baking powder

1. Preheat oven to 150°C (300°F). Beat **1** until soft peak forms. Puree **3** in juicer. Sift **4**.
2. Beat **2** until sugar dissolves, blend in vegetable oil, **3**, and **4** together. Add **1** and mix well.
3. Pour the batter into a 23 x 25cm (8"x10") lined square baking pan (illus. 1). Bake for 25 minutes. Remove and leave to cool.
4. Slice the cake to half (illus. 2), spread with a thick layer of jam filling and put back the other half (illus. 3).

■ American Orange Cake: Replace **3** with 1⅓ oz.(40 g) concentrated orange juice. Use mamalade instead of strawberry jam. The rest remains the same as above.

■ American Chocolate Cake: Replace **3** with 1⅓ oz.(40 g) chocolate fudge. Use butter cream instead of strawberry jam. The rest remains the same as above.

檸檬蛋糕 · Lemon Chocolate Cakes

檸檬巧克力(半塊)	500公克
檸檬汁	50公克
蘭姆酒	1½小匙
蛋	3個
1 糖粉	170公克
瑪琪琳	60公克
奶油	60公克
2 低筋麵粉	150公克
泡打粉	1小匙

1. 烤箱預熱至160℃；**1** 料打至鬆發後（約原量1倍以上），將蛋分次加入攪拌呈糊狀，再入過篩之 **2** 料輕輕拌勻，最後入蘭姆酒及檸檬汁拌勻即為麵糊。
2. 取檸檬模型塗上沙拉油並撒上一層薄麵粉後，將麵糊裝入擠花袋中均勻擠於模型內（約12－15個）（圖1），入烤箱烤約15分鐘，取出待涼備用。
3. 將檸檬巧克力置於鋼盆內，隔水加熱至溶化後（圖2），再取蛋糕沾裹檸檬巧克力（圖3），待其凝固即可。

1 lb. (500 g)	lemon chocolate (half block)
3⅓ T.	lemon juice
1½ t.	rum
3	eggs
1 6 oz. (170 g)	powdered sugar
2 oz. (60 g)	margarine
2 oz. (60 g)	butter
2 5⅓ oz. (150 g)	cake flour
1 t.	baking powder

1. Preheat oven to 160°C (320°F). Cream **1** until light and fluffy (the volume increases to double), add eggs one at a time. Gently blend in sifted **2**, add rum and lemon juice; mix well to become batter.
2. Grease lemon molds and dust with a thin layer of flour. Pipe the batter into the lemon molds (makes 12 to 15) (illus. 1). Bake for 15 minutes. Remove and leave to cool.
3. Melt lemon chocolate block over double boiler (illus. 2). Ice the cakes with melted lemon chocolate (illus. 3). Allow them to set.

臉譜蛋糕 · Small Decorative Cakes

奶水	75 公克
巧克力片	1 片
奶油霜	少許
① 細砂糖	112.5 公克
蛋	4 個
② 低筋麵粉	75 公克
泡打粉	1/4 小匙
ester S P	37.5 公克

1. 烤箱預熱至２００℃；２３×２５公分之方形烤盤抹油並撒上一層薄麵粉備用（圖１）。
2. ❶料打至糖溶化，入❷料攪拌約２至３分鐘後，續入奶水拌勻，裝入擠花袋中擠在烤盤上，使之呈小圓形狀（圖２），再入烤箱中層烤熟（約１２分鐘），取出待涼後，取２片小蛋糕合併，中間塗上奶油霜（作法見50頁）當夾心。（圖３）
3. 巧克力置鋼盆內，隔水加熱至溶化後，裝入擠花袋中，再將巧克力擠於蛋糕表面呈臉譜狀即可。

1/3 C. evaporated milk
1 block chocolate
as needed butter cream

① 4 oz. (112.5 g) granulated sugar
　 4 eggs

② 2 2/3 oz. (75 g) cake flour
　 1/4 t. baking powder
　 1 1/3 oz. (37.5 g) ester sp

1. Preheat oven to 200°C (390°F). Grease and flour 23x25cm(8"x10") baking pan. (illus. 1).
2. Whisk ❶ until sugar dissolves, add ❷ and beat for 2 to 3 minutes. Pour in milk and beat well. Pipe onto the baking sheet as small round cookies (illus. 2). Bake at the center rack of the oven for 12 minutes. Remove and leave them to cool. Sandwich two cookies together (illus. 3) with a layer of butter cream (ref. pg.50).
3. Melt the chocolate block over double boiler, place in a piping bag. Frost the cake sandwiches with funny faces.

千層蛋糕 • Layered Cake

低筋麵粉	110公克
果醬	一罐

1
- 蛋 .... 250公克（淨重）
- 細砂糖 125公克
- 鹽 1.5公克

2
- 沙拉油 35公克
- 奶水 35公克
- 蜂蜜 20公克

1. 烤箱預熱至２３０℃；２３×２５公分之方形烤盤鋪上蛋糕紙備用。
2. **1**料打發後（即手指勾起麵糊時可站立）（圖1），入過篩之低筋麵粉輕輕拌勻，再入**2**料拌勻即為麵糊。
3. 將¼麵糊倒入方形烤盤內，入烤箱烤４分鐘至著色後，再倒入第二層麵糊（圖２），續入烤箱烤４分鐘至著色，如此重覆四次，最後一次烤至熟後（約８分鐘），取出待涼。
4. 將蛋糕從中對切成二等分方形，一塊塗上果醬後，上鋪另一塊蛋糕，然後橫豎各切一刀成四等分，再將每等分依對角切半使成三角狀即可（圖3）。

- 4 oz. (110 g) cake flour
- 1 .... jar fruit jam

1
- 9 oz. (250 g) .... eggs (net weight)
- 4½ oz. (125 g) .... granulated sugar
- ¼ t. .... salt

2
- 1¼ oz. (35 g) .... vegetable oil
- 2⅓ T. .... evaporated milk
- ¾ oz. (20 g) .... honey

1. Preheat oven to 230°C (450°F). Line a 23 x 25cm (8"x10") square baking pan.
2. Beat **1** until soft peaks from (illus. 1), fold into sifted flour gently, then mix in **2** to become batter.
3. Pour ¼ of the batter into the square baking pan. Bake for 4 minutes to color the surface. Pour in the second layer (illus. 2) and bake for 4 minutes. Repeat 4 times or until batter runs out. Bake the top layer for 8 minutes. Remove and leave to cool.
4. Cut the cake to two equal rectangles. Spread a layer of jam on top of one cake. Put the other rectangle on top to sandwich the jam. Cut the cake to quarters and then to triangles (illus. 3); showing all the layers inside.

大理石蛋糕 · Marble Cake

蛋	2個
牛奶	50公克
可可粉	1大匙

1
- 奶油 .... 95 公克
- 細砂糖 .... 100 公克
- 香草精 .... 2 小匙

2
- 低筋麵粉 .... 113 公克
- 泡打粉 1小匙

1 烤箱預熱至１７５℃；９．５×１８．５×６．５公分之長方形模型內塗油並舖上蛋糕紙備用。
2 將❶料拌打均勻後，入蛋液打至乳白色，再入過篩之❷料拌勻，最後入牛奶拌勻即為麵糊。
3 取 1/3 麵糊加入可可粉拌勻後（圖１），將剩餘 2/3 麵糊分成兩半，一半倒入模型內，續入加可可粉之麵糊，最後入剩餘之白麵糊（圖２），再用竹籤畫出花紋（圖３），入烤箱烤３５分鐘即可。

2 .... eggs
3 1/3 T. milk or light cream
1 T. .... cocoa powder

1
- 3 1/3 oz. (95 g) butter or margarine
- 4 1/3 oz. (100 g) granulated sugar
- 2 t. .... vanilla essence

2
- 4 oz. (113 g) cake flour
- 1 t. .... baking powder

1 Preheat oven to 175°C (350°F). Grease and line a 9.5 x 18.5 x 6.5 cm (4" x 7" x 2 3/4") baking pan.
2 Cream ❶ ; then add beaten eggs and beat until light and fluffy. Beat in sifted ❷ to become batter, then add milk, blend well.
3 Put 1/3 of the batter into another bowl and mix in cocoa powder (illus. 1). Pour half of the white batter into the baking pan, then pour in the cocoa batter, and top with the other half of the white batter (illus. 2). Trail a stick lightly through the batter to produce the marble design (illus. 3). Bake for 35 minutes.

巧克力戚風蛋糕 · Chocolate Chiffon Cake

1
- 可可粉 ... 20 公克(13.3%)
- 熱水 .... 80 公克(53.3%)

2
- 低筋麵粉 150 公克(100%)
- 蘇打粉 .... 3 公克(1.9%)
- 細砂糖 . 100 公克(66.6%)
- 鹽 .... 2 公克(1.3%)

3
- 沙拉油 ..... 35公克(23.3%)
- 蛋黃 .... 50 公克 (33.3%)

4
- 蛋白 ...... 100 公克(56.6%)
- 細砂糖 ...... 85 公克(60%)
- 鹽 .... 0.5 公克(0.33%)

1　烤箱預熱至１７５℃；８寸模型內塗油並撒上一層薄麵粉；**1**料調勻；**2**料過篩攪拌均勻；**4**料打至乾性發泡備用。
2　**3**料與調勻之**2**料混合，續入**1**料拌勻，取**4**料的三分之一倒入輕輕拌勻後，倒回剩餘之**4**料中輕拌均勻即為麵糊。
3　將麵糊倒入模型內，入烤箱烤２０分鐘後，取出待涼，再用鮮奶油、巧克力屑、水果裝飾表面即可。

1
- $^{3}/_{4}$ oz. (20 g) .... cocoa powder (13.3%)
- $^{1}/_{3}$ C ....warm water(53.3 %)

2
- $5^{1}/_{3}$ oz. (150 g) ...... cake flour (100 %)
- $^{2}/_{3}$ t. baking soda (1.9%)
- $3^{1}/_{2}$ oz. (100 g) .. granulated sugar (66.6%)
- $^{1}/_{2}$ t. .... salt (1.3%)

3
- $1^{1}/_{4}$ oz. (35 g) .... vegetable oil (23.3%)
- $1^{3}/_{4}$ oz. (50 g) .... egg yolks (33.3%)

4
- $3^{1}/_{2}$ oz. (100 g) .... egg whites (56.6%)
- 3 oz. (85 g) granulated sugar (60%)
- $^{1}/_{8}$ t. .... salt (0.33%)

1　Preheat oven to 175°C (350°F). Grease and flour a 8" round mold. Mix **1**. Sift **2** together. Whisk **4** until stiff peaks form.
2　Gently mix **3** and **2**; pour in **1** and blend well. Fold in $^{1}/_{3}$ of **4**, then mix in the rest of **4** to become the batter.
3　Pour the batter into the mold and bake for 20 minutes. Remove and leave to cool. Frost with whipped cream.

香草戚風蛋糕 · Vanilla Chiffon Cake

低筋麵粉 ...... 150 公克(100%)
香草精 .... 1小匙(0.46%)

1
- 細砂糖 .. 50 公克(33.3 %)
- 泡打粉 .... 4.6公克(3%)
- 鹽 .... 0.5 公克

2
- 蛋黃 ...... 100 公克(66.6 %)
- 奶水 .... 90 公克(59.9 %)
- 沙拉油 ... 70 公克(46.6%)

3
- 蛋白 ...... 200公克(133.3%)
- 細砂糖 .. 100公克(66.6%)
- 塔塔粉 ... 0.5公克(0.33%)

1. 烤箱預熱至１７５℃；8寸空心模型內塗油並撒上一層薄麵粉；低筋麵粉過篩後，與**1**料攪拌均勻；**3**料打至乾性發泡備用。
2. 將**2**料與調勻之**1**料混和，再取**3**料的 1/3 倒入輕輕拌勻後，倒回剩餘之**3**料中輕拌均勻即為麵糊。
3. 將麵糊倒入模型內，入烤箱烤２０分鐘後，取出待涼，再用鮮奶油、水蜜桃裝飾表面即可。

5 1/3 oz. (150 g) cake flour (100%)
1 t. vanilla extract (0.46%)

1
- 1 3/4 oz.(50g)........... granulated sugar (33.3%)
- 1 t. baking powder (3%)
- 1/8 t. salt

2
- 3 1/2 oz. (100 g) .... egg yolks, about 6 (66.6%)
- 3 1/4 oz. (90 g) .... evaporated milk (59.9%)
- 2 1/2 oz. (70 g) vegetable oil (46.6%)

3
- 7 oz. (200 g) egg whites, about 6 (133.3%)
- 3 1/2 oz. (100 g) .. granulated sugar(66.6%)
- 1/8 t. cream of tartar (0.33%)

1. Preheat oven to 175 °C (350° F). Grease and flour a 8 " ring mold. Sift cake flour and mix well with **1**. Whisk **3** until soft peaks form.
2. Mix **2** and **1**, fold in 1/3 of **3**. Then mix in the rest of **3** to become the batter.
3. Pour the batter into the mold, bake in the oven for 20 minutes. Remove and leave to cool. Frost with whipped cream.

迷你卡通蛋糕 · Mini Cartoon Cakes

奶水、蜂蜜各 20公克
巧克力 ..... （半塊）500公克
奶油霜 .... 少許

1 ⎡ 蛋 100公克
　 ⎣ 細砂糖 60公克

2 ⎡ 低筋麵粉 40公克
　 ⎣ 玉米粉 10公克

1. 烤箱預熱至150℃；23×25公分之方形烤盤鋪上蛋糕紙備用。
2. **1**料打至鬆發（約3倍量），入過篩之**2**料拌勻，再入奶水、蜂蜜攪拌均勻後，倒入烤盤內，入烤箱烤熟（約8分鐘），取出待涼。
3. 將蛋糕捲成圓柱狀，接口處塗上奶油霜（圖1），放置15分鐘使其定型後，切6公分長度，橫切面再用圓形擠花嘴擠上奶油霜（圖2），置冰箱冷藏使之凝固。
4. 巧克力切碎置鋼盆內，隔水加熱至溶化後即為巧克力醬。
5. 將蛋糕上之奶油霜沾滿巧克力醬（圖3），再用各色奶油裝點成眼睛、口、鼻即可。

1 1/3 T. each: evaporated milk, honey
17 2/3 oz. (500 g) baking chocolate (half block)
as needed butter cream

1 ⎡ 3 1/2 oz. (100 g) ...... eggs
　 ⎣ 2 1/4 oz. (60 g) .... granulated sugar

2 ⎡ 3 1/2 oz. (40 g) cake flour
　 ⎣ 1/3 oz. (10 g) corn flour

1. Preheat oven to 150°C (300°F). Line a 23x25cm (8"x10") square baking mold.
2. Beat **1** until frothy (volume increases by three times). Blend in sifted **2**. Pour in milk and honey, mix well. Pour the mixture into the mold, bake for 8 minutes. Remove and leave to cool.
3. Roll the cake into a cylinder, seal with butter cream (illus. 1). Let it stand for 15 minutes to set. Cut every 6 cm (2 1/2") and pipe butter cream on the round surfaces (illus. 2). Stand in refrigerator to set.
4. Melt chocolate in a double boiler.
5. Spread chocolate fudge over the butter cream (illus. 3). Draw on eyes, noses, and mouths with different colors of cream.

巴巴樂蛋糕 · Bavarian Cream with Fruits

鮮奶油	....	275 公克
檸檬汁	....	22 公克
水蜜桃	....	適量
紅櫻桃	....	適量
❶	水	340 公克
	細砂糖	105 公克
❷	水	85 公克
	吉利丁	17 公克
❸	鮮奶	340 公克
	蛋黃	85 公克
	細砂糖	60 公克
❹	鮮奶	85 公克
	吉利丁	17 公克

1. ❶料拌勻煮開，入❷料續煮至吉利丁融化後，分成二等份，一份倒入１０吋模型內，入冰箱冷藏至固體狀（圖１），取出，排上水蜜桃及紅櫻桃，再入另一半吉利丁液（圖２），置冰箱冷藏備用。
2. ❸料煮開後拌入❹料，待涼，入打發之鮮奶油與檸檬汁拌勻，倒入已凝固之吉利丁上抹平（圖３），再入冰箱冷藏至固體狀即可。

9 3/4 oz. (275 g) fresh cream
1 1/2 T. .... lemon juice
as needed canned peaches
as needed red cherries

❶	1 1/3 C. .... water
	3 3/4 oz. (105 g) .... granulated sugar
❷	1/3 C. .... water
	2/3 oz.(17 g) .... gelatin
❸	1 1/3 C. .... milk
	3 oz. (85 g) ...egg yolks
	2 oz. (60 g) .... granulated sugar
❹	1/3 C. .... milk
	2/3 oz. (17 g) .... gelatin

1. Bring ❶ to a boil, add ❷ and boil until gelatin dissolves. Pour half into a 10" mold and refrigerate until set (illus. 1). Remove from refrigerator, put a layer of peaches and cherries on, then pour over the other half of gelatin mixture (illus. 2). Set in refrigerator.
2. Bring ❸ to a boil, then add ❹; leave to cool. Fold in whipped cream and lemon juice. Pour over set bavarian and smooth it (illus. 3). Leave in refrigerator until set.

葡萄戚風捲 · Raisin Swiss Roll

蛋白	150公克
細砂糖	70公克
葡萄乾	60公克
沙拉油	40公克
奶水	30公克
蛋黃	4個
塔塔粉	1/8 小匙
奶油霜	少許
香草精	1/4 小匙

❶ 低筋麵粉 65公克
　　泡打粉 2公克

❷ 細砂糖 30公克
　　鹽 .... 1/3 小匙

1. 烤箱預熱至170℃；23×25公分之方形烤盤鋪上蛋糕紙備用。（圖1）
2. 香草精與過篩之❶、❷料混合均勻，再依序入沙拉油、蛋黃、奶水拌勻備用。
3. 蛋白與塔塔粉打至起泡，再入細砂糖打至濕性發泡後，與作法1之材料輕輕拌勻，續入葡萄乾攪拌均勻，倒入烤盤內，入烤箱中層烤10分鐘後，移至上層，改以120℃再烤10分鐘，最後移至中層，續以170℃烤2分鐘後，取出待涼。
4. 蛋糕表面塗上奶油霜後（圖2），除去蛋糕紙並捲成圓筒狀即可（圖3）。

5 1/3 oz. (150 g) .. egg whites
2 1/2 oz. (70 g) granulated sugar
2 oz. (60 g) .... raisins
2 1/2 T. .... vegetable oil
2 T. .... evaporated milk
4 .... egg yolks
1/8 t. .... cream of tartar
as needed butter cream
1/4 t. .... vanilla extract

❶ 2 1/3 oz. (65 g) cake flour
　　1/2 t. ..... baking powder

❷ 1 oz. (30 g) ....
　　granulated sugar
　　1/3 t. .... salt

1. Preheat oven to 170°C (340°F). Line a 23x25cm (8"x10") square baking pan (illus. 1).
2. Mix vanilla extract and sifted ❶, ❷ ; mix well. Then add oil, egg yolks, and evaporated milk; blend well.
3. Whisk egg whites and cream of tartar until frothy, add sugar and beat until soft peaks form. Gently mix in the egg yolk mixture. Stir in raisins. Pour the batter into the baking pan. Bake at the center of oven for 10 minutes. Then bake on the upper rack at 120°C (250°F) for 10 minutes. Bake again at the center at 170°C (340°F) for 2 minutes. Remove and leave to cool.
4. Spread with a layer of butter cream (illus. 2). Remove the lining paper and roll into cylinder. (illus. 3)

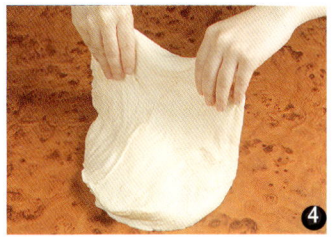  

軟式甜麵糰 · Basic Sweet Roll Dough

高筋麵粉 .... 350 公克
奶油 .... 40 公克

1
- 高筋麵粉 .... 150 公克
- 鹽 .... 5 公克

2
- 水 .... 175 公克
- 細砂糖 .... 15 公克
- 乾酵母 .... 5 公克
- 蛋 .... 1 個

3
- 水 .... 90-95 公克
- 細砂糖 .... 85 公克
- 奶粉 .... 10 公克
- 乾酵母 .... 5 公克

1 高筋麵粉過篩後，置不銹鋼盆或陶磁大碗內（圖1）；奶油置室溫下軟化；**1**料過篩備用。
2 **2**料拌勻，倒入高筋麵粉內揉勻，蓋上扭乾之濕布（使麵糰保濕）（圖2），放在溫暖潮濕的地方發酵1小時後，入拌勻之**3**料揉勻，再入**1**料搓揉均勻，最後將奶油分2至3次入麵糰內揉勻（圖3）。
3 將麵糰拿起，往下摔打，對折後（圖4），換邊握住再摔打一下（圖5），以此方法連續摔打至麵糰光滑後（圖6）（約200次），再蓋上扭乾之濕布鬆弛10分鐘，即爲軟式甜麵糰。

■ 材料中水的部份，依天氣溫度作調整；夏天使用冰水，爲避免溫度太高，發酵太快或無法發酵，甚至可加點冰塊，冬天則用冷水即可。

12 1/3 oz. (350 g) bread flour
1 2/5 oz. (40g) butter or margarine

1
- 5 1/3 oz. (150 g) bread flour
- 1 t. salt

2
- 3/4 C. water
- 1/2 oz. (15 g) granulated sugar
- 1 t. active dry yeast
- 1 egg

3
- 2/5 C. water
- 3 oz. (85 g) granulated sugar
- 1/3 oz. (10 g) milk powder
- 1 t. active dry yeast

1 Into large bowl, sift flour (illus. 1). Soften butter or margarine at room temperature. Sift **1**.
2 Beat **2**, pour into sifted flour and knead. Cover with a damp cloth (illus. 2) and let it rise in a warm place for one hour. Add well-mixed **3** Knead in **1**, then knead in butter or margarine, half or one third at a time (illus. 3) until well blended.
3 Throw the dough against a board or table for a few times. Fold into half (illus. 4), and again throw once on the other side (illus. 5). Repeat this until the dough becomes smooth and shiny (illus. 6) (about 200 times). Cover again with a damp cloth and let it rest for 10 minutes. This is the basic sweet roll dough.

■ The temperature for the water should be adjusted according to the weather. Use ice water during the summer to prevent rising too fast or does not rise enough; even add ice cubes if necessary. Use cold water during the winter months.

熱狗捲 · Hot Dogs in Buns

軟式甜麵糰	1份
熱狗	16支
番茄醬	適量

1. 烤箱預熱至１８０℃備用。
2. 麵糰分成１６等份，用手搓圓後，蓋上扭乾之濕布鬆弛１０分鐘。
3. 每個小麵糰搓成２０－２５公分長之棒狀，再疏鬆的盤旋在熱狗上（圖１），熱狗兩端各露出１－２公分，麵糰兩端塞到裡面（圖２），接縫處朝下置於塗有奶油之烤盤上，麵糰間隔４－５公分，蓋上扭乾之濕布，放在溫暖潮濕的地方發酵至２倍大（約９０分鐘）。
4. 取一塑膠袋，裝入番茄醬後，從袋角剪一小缺口，在麵糰上擠上線條（圖３），入烤箱烤至上色（約１４－１５分鐘），取出時連同烤盤輕摔一下，麵包表面再趁熱塗上奶油即可。

1 .... quantity basic sweet roll dough
16 .... hot dogs
as needed catsup

1. Preheat oven to 180°C (355°F).
2. Divide the dough into 16 equal portions and roll into balls. Cover with damp cloth and let rest for 10 minutes.
3. Roll each ball into 20 - 25 cm (8") long strip, loosely circle around a hot dog (illus. 1); leave both hot dog tips out about 1 - 2 cm. Tuck in the dough ends (illus. 2) and the opening side underneath. Place the rolls on a greased baking sheet with 4 - 5 cm (2") space in between. Cover with a damp cloth and let rise in a warm, damp place until the bulk doubled (about 90 minutes).
4. Place catsup in a piping bag and pipe onto the rolls (illus. 3). Bake until golden (about 14 - 15 minutes). Remove from oven and knock the baking sheet against a table for easy removal of the rolls. Brush tops of buns with butter or margarine while still warm.

蘋果麵包捲 · Apple Rolls

軟式甜麵糰	一份
小蘋果	3個(約550公克)
高筋麵粉	少許

1
- 細砂糖 .... 3½ 大匙
- 水 .... 3½ 大匙
- 檸檬汁 1小匙

2
- 細砂糖 .... 3½ 小匙
- 肉桂粉 1小匙

1 烤箱預熱至１９０℃備用。
2 蘋果去皮，切成０·７公分細小丁置不銹鋼鍋內，與 **1** 料拌勻後，蓋上鍋蓋用中火先煮５分鐘，等蘋果變黃時，打開鍋蓋，待湯汁收乾，盛起待涼即為蘋果餡。
3 麵糰上均勻撒些高筋麵粉，再用擀麵棍擀成３０×３０公分正方形（圖１），撒上拌勻之 **2** 料及蘋果餡（圖２），再將麵糰密實的捲成圓柱狀，接縫處捏緊置下方，然後切成２公分寬之圓片（圖３），置於塗油之烤盤上，麵糰間隔４至５公分，蓋上扭乾之濕布，放在溫暖潮濕的地方發酵至２倍大（約９０分鐘）。
4 將麵糰入烤箱烤至上色（約１０分鐘），取出時連同烤盤輕摔一下，麵包表面再趁熱塗上奶油即可。

1 .... quantity basic sweet roll dough
3 (about 1⅕ lb.) .... apples
as needed bread flour

1
- 3½ T. .... granulated sugar
- 3½ T. .... water
- 1 t. .... lemon juice

2
- 3½ t. granulated sugar
- 1 t. cinnamon powder

1 Preheat oven to 190°C (375°F).
2 Peel the apples and dice to 0.7 cm (¾") cubes. Place diced apples in a stainless pot and mix well with **1** ; cover and cook over medium heat for 5 minutes. Remove the lid and beat until liquid evaporates ; remove and leave to cool. This is the apple filling.
3 Dust some bread flour on the basic sweet roll dough, roll it out to 30 cm x 30cm (12" x12") square (illus. 1). Sprinkle on well-mixed **2** and apple filling (illus. 2). Roll the dough tightly into a cylinder, press in the opening and tuck it under; then cut it into 2 cm (1") wide rounds (illus. 3). Place them on a greased baking sheet with 4-5cm (1½" -2") space in between. Cover with a damp cloth and let rise in a warm, damp place until the bulk doubled (about 90minutes).
4 Bake until golden (about 10 minutes). Remove from oven and knock the baking sheet lightly against the table for easy removal of the rolls. Brush tops of rolls with butter or margarine while still warm.

椰子玉米麵包 · Corn - Coconut Buns

軟式甜麵糰 1份
玉米粒 1罐
美乃滋 225公克
奶油、蛋液 各60公克

1
椰子粉 120公克
糖粉 120公克
奶粉 60公克

1. 烤箱預熱至180℃；**1**料拌勻，入蛋液打勻後，再入奶油揉勻，分成16等份即為內餡。
2. 麵糰分成16等份，用手搓圓，蓋上扭乾之濕布鬆弛10分鐘。
3. 取一份麵糰，壓扁後包入一份內餡，收口處捏緊朝上，用擀麵棍擀成橢圓形後，由上往下密實的捲起，接縫處捏緊朝下，置於塗有奶油之烤盤上，麵糰間隔4－5公分，再用剪刀或小刀從麵糰中間劃開（圖1）（頭尾須留2至3公分），蓋上扭乾之濕布，放在溫暖潮濕的地方發酵至2倍大（約90分鐘）。
4. 在每個麵糰劃開處撒上1大匙玉米粒（圖2），並擠上適量之美乃滋後（圖3），入烤箱烤至上色（約15－18分鐘），取出時連同烤盤輕摔一下，麵包表面再趁熱塗上奶油即可。

1 .... quantity basic sweet roll dough
1 .... can corn
8 oz. (225 g) .. mayonnaise
2oz. (60 g) each: butter or margarine, beaten eggs

1
4½ oz. (120 g) .... desiccated coconut
4½ oz. (120 g) .... powdered sugar
2 oz. (60 g) .... milk powder

1. Preheat oven to 180°C (355°F). Beat the egg and mixture **1**. Knead in butter or margarine. Divide into 16 equal portions. This is the coconut filling.
2. Divide the basic sweet roll dough into 16 equal portions, and roll into balls. Cover with a damp cloth and let rest for 10 minutes.
3. Lightly press each dough flat, wrap a portion of filling inside. Press in the opening and leave it facing upward. Roll out into oblong shape. Roll into a cylinder lengthwise. Place seam side down 4 - 5 cm (1 ½"-2") apart on a greased baking sheet. Snip, with a scissor or small knife, open in the center (illus. 1). Cover with a damp cloth and let rise in a warm, damp place until the bulk has doubled (about 90 minutes).
4. Sprinkle 1 T. corn into the slits on top (illus. 2) and pipe on mayonnaise (illus. 3). Bake until golden (about 15 - 18 minutes). Remove from oven and knock the baking sheet against a table for easy removal of the buns. Brush top of buns with butter or margarine while still warm.

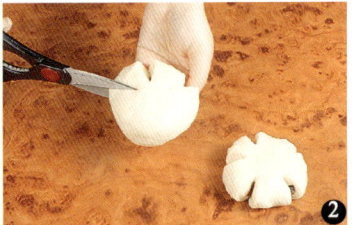

紅豆麵包 · Rolls with Red Bean Filling

軟式甜麵糰 1份
紅豆餡 500公克
蛋 1個

1. 烤箱預熱至１８０℃；紅豆餡分成１６等份備用（紅豆餡作法請參見紅豆多拿滋）。
2. 麵糰分成１６等份，用手搓圓，蓋上扭乾之濕布鬆弛１０分鐘。
3. 取一份麵糰，壓扁後包入一份紅豆餡，收口後把麵糰稍壓扁（圖１），用剪刀在邊緣均勻剪上５刀（圖２），置於塗有奶油之烤盤上，蓋上扭乾之濕布，放在溫暖潮濕的地方發酵至２倍大（約９０分鐘）。
4. 將發酵好之麵糰刷上蛋液（圖３），入烤箱烤至上色（約１０－１５分鐘），取出時連同烤盤輕摔一下，麵包表面再趁熱塗上奶油即可。

1 .... quantity basic sweet roll dough
1 1/6 lb. (500 g) red bean filling
1 .... egg
as needed butter or margarine

1. Preheat oven to 180°C (355°F). Divide the red bean filling into 16 equal portions (ref. Doughnuts with Red Bean filling).
2. Divide the dough into 16 equal portions, roll into balls and cover with damp cloth, let rest for 10 minutes.
3. Flatten each ball and wrap a portion of red bean filling inside. Pinch to seal and press slightly to flatten (illus. 1). With a scissor, snip the edge 5 times (illus. 2). Place the rolls on a greased baking sheet and cover with a damp cloth. Place in a warm, damp place until the bulk has doubled (about 90 minutes).
4. Brush the rolls with beaten egg (illus. 3) and bake until golden (about 10 - 15 minutes). Remove from the oven and knock the baking sheet against a table for easy removal of the rolls. Brush tops of rolls with butter or margarine while still warm.

乳酪麵包 · Ham - Cheese Buns

軟式甜麵糰 1份
火腿 16片
起司片 8片

1 烤箱預熱至１８０℃備用。
2 將麵糰分成１６等份，用手搓圓，蓋上扭乾之濕布鬆弛１０分鐘。
3 每個小麵糰用擀麵棍擀成直徑１２公分的圓片，放上一片火腿及半片起司，再把麵糰由上往下捲起（圖１），接縫處捏緊對折後，從對折處切開 ²/₃ 長度（圖２），再從切開的地方拉開攤平，置於塗有奶油之烤盤上，蓋上扭乾之濕布，放在溫暖潮濕的地方發酵至２倍大（約９０分鐘）。
4 將麵糰入烤箱烤至上色（約１４－１５分鐘），取出時連同烤盤輕摔一下，麵包表面再趁熱塗上奶油即可（圖３）。

1 .... quantity basic sweet roll dough
16 .... slices ham
8 ..... slices cheddar cheese

1 Preheat oven to 180°C (355 °F).
2 Divide the dough into 16 equal portions. Roll into balls and cover with a damp cloth for 10 minutes.
3 Roll each ball out with a rolling pin to 12 cm (4") round pieces. Place a piece of ham and half piece of cheese on top. Roll the dough from upper side downward (illus. 1). Press to seal the openings and fold to half. With sharp knife, cut ²/₃ of the length at the fold (illus. 2). Then spread out the slits. Place the buns on a greased baking sheet. Cover with a damp cloth and let rise in a warm, damp place until the bulk has doubled (about 90 minutes).
4 Bake until golden (about 14 - 15 minutes). Remove from oven and knock the baking sheet against a table for easy removal of the buns. Brush tops of hot buns with butter or margarine while still warm (illus. 3).

玉米火腿麵包 · Corn - Ham Buns

軟式甜麵糰 1份
玉米、青豆仁 各150公克
洋火腿 16片
美乃滋 .... 適量

1. 烤箱預熱至１８０℃；麵糰分成１６等份，用手搓圓，蓋上扭乾之濕布鬆弛１０分鐘。
2. 將麵糰擀成直徑１０－１２公分寬之圓片，放上一片火腿，再由上往下密實的捲起（圖１），接縫處捏緊對折後，從對折處切開 ²/₃ 長度（圖２），再從切開的地方拉開攤平（圖３），置於塗有沙拉油之烤盤上，蓋上扭乾之濕布，放在溫暖潮濕的地方發酵至２倍大（約９０分鐘）。
3. 每個麵糰上先擠上約２小匙的美乃滋，再放上混合均勻的玉米青豆仁，最後擠上少許美奶滋作裝飾。
4. 將麵糰入烤箱烤至上色（約１４至１５分鐘）；取出時連同烤盤輕摔一下，麵包表面再趁熱塗上奶油即可。

---

1 .... quantity basic sweet roll dough
5¹/₂ oz.(150 g) each: canned corn, green peas
16 .... slices ham
as needed mayonnaise

1. Preheat oven to 180°C (355°F). Divide the dough into 16 equal portions, roll into balls. Cover with a damp cloth and let rest for 10 minutes.
2. Roll each ball with a rolling pin into 10 - 12 cm (4") wide round pieces. Place a piece of ham on top, then roll from upper end downward tightly (illus. 1). Press to seal the opening and fold to half. With sharp knife, cut ²/₃ of the length at the fold (illus. 2). Then spread out the slits (illus. 3). Place the buns on a greased baking sheet and cover with a damp cloth. Let them rise in a warm, damp place until the bulk has doubled (about 90 minutes).
3. Pipe 2t. mayonnaise onto each bun and put on mixed corns and green peas. Decorate the top with a little more mayonnaise.
4. Bake until golden (about 14 - 15 minutes). Remove from oven and knock the baking sheet on a table for easy removal of the buns. Brush tops of hot buns with butter or margarine while still warm.

地瓜麵包 · Rolls with Yam Filling

軟式甜麵糰	1份
地瓜	560公克
細砂糖	1½ 大匙
①　細砂糖	60公克
奶油	30公克
罐頭鳳梨	½ 片

1. 烤箱預熱至180℃；奶油置室溫下軟化；鳳梨切碎備用（圖1）。
2. 地瓜去皮，切2公分厚片，用大火蒸熟（約20－25分鐘），取出後壓成泥並趁熱拌上❶料即為地瓜餡，分成16等份待涼備用。
3. 麵糰分成16等份，用手搓圓後，蓋上扭乾之濕布（圖2）鬆弛10分鐘。
4. 取一份麵糰，壓扁後包入一份地瓜餡，然後收口處捏緊朝上，置於塗油之烤盤內，麵糰間隔4－5公分，蓋上扭乾之濕布，放在溫暖潮濕的地方發酵至2倍大（約90分鐘）。
5. 每個麵糰上撒⅓小匙的細砂糖（圖3），再入烤箱烤至上色（約14－15分鐘），取出時連同烤盤輕摔一下，麵包表面再趁熱塗上奶油即可。

1	quantity basic sweet roll dough
1⅕ lb. (560 g)	yam
1½ T.	granulated sugar
①　2 oz. (60 g)	granulated sugar
1 oz. (30 g)	butter or margarine
½	slice canned pineapple

1. Preheat oven to 180°C (355°F). Soften butter or margarine at room temperature. Chop pineapple finely (illus. 1).
2. Peel off yam skin and cut into 2 cm (1") thick slices. Steam over high heat until cooked (about 20 - 25 minutes). Remove and mash to yam paste; mix with while still warm. ❶ This is the yam filling. Divide the filling into 16 equal portions.
3. Divide the dough into 16 equal portions, knead into balls. Cover with a damp cloth (illus. 2) and let them rest for 10 minutes.
4. Press on each balls to flatten into rounds, wrap a portion of filling inside. Seal the opening facing upward. Place them on a greased baking sheet 4 - 5 cm (1½" - 2") apart. Cover with a damp cloth and leave in a warm, damp place to rise until doubled (about 90 minutes).
5. Sprinkle ⅓ t. granulated sugar on top of each roll (illus. 3). Bake until golden (about 14 - 15 minutes). Remove from oven and knock the baking sheet against the table for easy removal of the rolls. Brush tops of rolls with butter or margarine while still warm.

香脆馬鈴薯麵包 · Potato and Cheese Rolls

軟式甜麵糰 1份
馬鈴薯 500公克
起司絲 480公克

1 烤箱預熱至１８０℃；馬鈴薯洗淨，加水４杯煮熟後（約３５－４５分鐘），撈起去皮，切成０．５公分細小丁，分１６等份待涼備用。
2 麵糰分成１６等份，用手搓圓，置桌面上並蓋上扭乾之濕布鬆弛１０分鐘。
3 取一份麵糰，壓扁後包入一份馬鈴薯及１大匙起司絲（圖１），然後收口處捏緊朝下，置於塗油之烤盤上，麵糰間隔４至５公分，蓋上扭乾之濕布，放在溫暖潮濕的地方發酵至２倍大（約９０分鐘）。
4 每個麵糰上撒１大匙起司絲（圖２），再入烤箱烤至上色（約１４－１５分鐘），取出時連同烤盤輕摔一下，麵包表面再趁熱塗上奶油即可。

■ 若烤盤容量太小，無法將麵糰全部放進去時，可將錫箔紙裁成１０公分平方（圖３），再把麵糰放在上面進行發酵，發酵完成後，連同錫箔紙一起入烤箱，以避免黏在容器上而導致變形。

1 .... quantity basic sweet roll dough
1 1/6 lb. (500 g) ..... potatoes
1 lb. (480 g) .... shredded cheese

1 Preheat oven to 180°C (355°F). Wash the potatoes and boil in 4 C. water until done (about 35 - 45 minutes); remove and peel off the skin, dice into 0.5 cm (1/4") cubes. Divide diced potatoes into 16 equal portions and leave to cool.
2 Divide the dough into 16 equal portions, knead into balls. Cover with a damp cloth and let them rest for 10 minutes.
3 Press each dough ball flat. Wrap a portion of potato and 1 T. shredded cheese into each piece of dough (illus. 1). Tuck the opening underneath. Place on a greased baking sheet 4 - 5 cm (1 1/2" - 2 ") apart. Cover with a damp cloth and leave to rise in a warm, damp place until doubled (about 90 minutes).
4 Sprinkle 1 T. shredded cheese on top of each roll (illus. 2). Bake until golden (about 14 - 15 minutes). Remove from oven and knock the baking sheet against a table for easy removal of the rolls. Brush the tops with butter or margarine while still warm.

■ If the baking sheet is too small to accommodate all the rolls, each roll may be placed on a 10 cm greased foil paper square (illus. 3). After raising to double, bake in oven with foil paper to prevent sticking.

布丁餡甜麵包 · Custard Filled Rolls

軟式甜麵糰 .... 1 份
美乃滋 .... 1/2 杯

布丁餡：
鮮奶 .... 200 公克
細砂糖 .... 35 公克
玉米粉 .... 30 公克
低筋麵粉 .... 25 公克
奶油 .... 15 公克
蛋 .... 1 個

1. 烤箱預熱至１８０℃；布丁餡作法請參照「奶油泡芙」之作法１，待餡冷卻後，分成１６等份備用。
2. 麵糰分成１６等份，用手搓圓（圖１），置桌面並蓋上扭乾之濕布鬆弛１０分鐘（圖２）。
3. 取一份麵糰，壓扁後包入一份布丁餡，收口處捏緊朝下，置於塗有奶油之烤盤上，麵糰間隔４－５公分，蓋上扭乾之濕布，放在溫暖潮濕的地方發酵至２倍大（約９０分鐘）。
4. 將美乃滋擠於麵糰上使成螺旋狀（圖３），再入烤箱烤至麵包上色（約１４－１５分鐘），取出時連同烤盤輕摔一下即可。

1 .... quantity basic sweet roll dough
1/2 C. .... mayonnaise

custard filling:
4/5 C. .... fresh milk
1 1/2 oz. (35 g) ... granulated sugar
1 oz. (30 g) .... corn flour
1 oz. (25 g) .... cake flour
1/2 oz. (15 g) ....
butter or margarine
1 .... egg

1. Preheat oven to 180°C (355°F). Prepare custard filling as Cream Puffs (page26), step 1. Divide the filling into 16 equal portions after cooled.
2. Divide the dough into 16 equal portions, shape into a ball (illus. 1). Cover with damp cloth and let rest for 10 minutes (illus. 2).
3. Flatten each piece of dough and wrap a portion of filling inside. Pinch to seal with the end underneath. Place them on a greased baking sheet 4 - 5 cm (1 1/2" - 2 ") apart. Cover with a damp cloth and let rise in a warm, damp place until doubled (about 90 minutes).
4. Pipe mayonnaise spirally onto the rolls (illus. 3). Bake until golden (about 14 - 15 minutes). Remove from the oven and knock the baking sheet against a table for easy removal of the rolls.

橄欖形餐包 · Oblong Dinner Rolls

軟式甜麵糰 .... 1/2 份
蛋 .... 1 個
奶油 .... 適量

1 烤箱預熱至１８０℃；奶油置室溫下軟化；蛋打勻備用。
2 麵糰分成１６等份，用手搓圓（圖１），蓋上扭乾之濕布鬆弛１０分鐘（圖２）。
3 取一份麵糰，壓扁後包入１小匙奶油，收口處捏緊朝下，用手搓成橄欖形後，置於塗有奶油之烤盤上，蓋上扭乾之濕布放在溫暖潮濕的地方發酵至２倍大（約９０分鐘）。
4 將發酵好之麵糰刷上蛋液，再入烤箱烤至上色（約８－１０分鐘），取出時連同烤盤輕摔一下，麵包表面再趁熱塗上奶油即可（圖３）。

1/2 .... quantity basic sweet roll dough
1 .... egg
as needed butter or margarine

1 Preheat oven to 180°C (355°F). Soften butter or margarine at room temperature. Beat the egg.
2 Divide the dough into 16 equal portions and roll into balls (illus. 1). Cover with damp cloth and let rest for 10 minutes (illus. 2).
3 Flatten each ball into a round piece. Wrap 1t. butter or margarine inside, press to seal and place the opening underneath. Form each dough into oblong shape by hand. Place the rolls on a greased baking sheet and cover with damp cloth. Let it rise in a warm, damp place until doubled (about 90 minutes).
4 Brush each roll with beaten egg and bake until golden (about 8 - 10 minutes). Remove from the oven and knock the baking sheet against a table for easy removal of the rolls. Brush the tops with butter while still warm (illus. 3).

蘋果沙拉麵包 · Buns with Apple Salad Filling

軟式甜麵糰	1份
蘋果	550公克
馬鈴薯	300公克
火腿	150公克
小黃瓜	1條
1 美乃滋	6大匙
鹽、胡椒粉	各少許
奶油	少許

1. 烤箱預熱至１８０℃；馬鈴薯加水５杯用大火煮熟後，撈起去皮切成細小丁待涼；小黃瓜切細小丁，加少許鹽拌醃後，洗去鹽份；蘋果洗淨去皮及籽，亦切成細小丁泡在５％鹽水裡，瀝乾；火腿切細小丁備用。
2. 將馬鈴薯、蘋果、火腿、小黃瓜及 **1** 料拌勻後，放入冰箱冷藏即為沙拉。
3. 麵糰分成１６等份，用手搓圓，蓋上扭乾之濕布鬆弛１０分鐘，再用擀麵棍擀成長約２０至２５公分之橢圓型片狀（圖１），再由上往下將麵糰密實的捲起（圖２），接縫處捏緊朝下置於抹有奶油之烤盤上；麵糰間隔４至５公分；蓋上扭乾之濕布，放在溫暖潮濕的地方發酵至２倍大（約９０分鐘）。
4. 將麵糰入烤箱烤至上色（約１０－１２分鐘），取出時連同烤盤輕摔一下，麵包表面再趁熱塗上奶油，待冷卻後，從中間橫切開（但不可切斷）（圖３）並抹上少許奶油，最後夾入沙拉即可。

1	quantity basic sweet roll dough
1 1/5 lb. (550 g)	apples
11 oz.(300 g)	potatoes
5 1/2 oz. (150 g)	baby cucumber
1 6 T.	mayonnaise
dash each salt, pepper as needed	butter or margarine

1. Preheat oven to 180°C (355°F). Boil the potatoes in 5C. water until cooked. Remove, peel off the skin and dice, leave to cool. Dice the cucumbers, sprinkle on a little salt, rinse and pat dry. Peel the skin off the apples, discard the cores and dice; soak in 5% salt water, drain and pat dry. Dice the ham.
2. Mix potatoes, apples, ham, cucumbers and **1**; chill in refrigerator. This is the apple salad filling.
3. Divide the dough into 16 equal portions, shape each piece into a ball. Cover with a damp cloth for 10 minutes. Roll out the balls into 20 - 25 cm (8"- 10") oblong pieces (illus. 1). Roll the piece from upper side downward tightly (illus. 2). Press to seal the opening and place the opening underneath. Place the buns on a greased baking sheet 4 - 5 cm (1 1/2" - 2 ") apart. Cover with a damp cloth and let rise in a warm, damp place until the bulk doubled (about 90 minutes).
4. Bake until golden (about 10 - 12 minutes). Remove from oven and knock the baking sheet against a table for easy removal of the buns. Brush the tops with butter or margarine while still warm. Leave the buns to cool. Slit the center open (do not cut through) to form a pocket (illus. 3). Spread with butter or margarine and fill with apple salad filling.

墨西哥麵包 · Mexican Sweet Rolls

軟式甜麵糊 1份
餡：
1. 酥油 120公克
   糖粉 120公克
   奶粉 180公克
   蛋液 30公克
   奶水 15公克

墨西哥麵包皮：
2. 糖粉 90公克
   酥油 50公克
   瑪琪琳 45公克

低筋麵粉、蛋液各95公克

1. 烤箱預熱至180℃；**1**料打發至酥油顏色變淡（圖1），入奶水及蛋液打勻，再加奶粉拌勻後，分成16等份即為內餡。
2. 麵糊分成16等份，用手搓圓（圖2），蓋上扭乾之濕布鬆弛10分鐘。
3. 取一份麵糊，壓扁後包入1份內餡，收口處捏緊朝下，置於塗有奶油之烤盤上；麵糊間隔4至5公分；蓋上扭乾之濕布，放在溫暖潮濕的地方發酵至2倍大（約90分鐘）。
4. **2**料打發至酥油、瑪琪琳顏色變淡，再入蛋液打勻至無顆粒狀後，續入低筋麵粉拌勻即為麵糊，裝入圓嘴擠花袋中備用。
5. 在每個發酵好之麵糊上擠上麵糊，使麵糊成螺旋狀後（圖3），入烤箱烤至上色（約15至18分鐘），取出時連同烤盤輕摔一下即可。

1 ...... quantity basic sweet roll dough

filling:
1. 4 1/4 oz. (120 g) butter oil substitute
   4 1/4 oz. (120 g) powdered sugar

   6 1/3 oz. (180 g) ...... milk powder
   1 oz. (30 g) beaten eggs
   1 T. .. evaporated milk

outer skin dough:
2. 3 oz. (90 g) .... powdered sugar
   1 1/2 oz. (50 g) ..... butter oil substitute
   1 1/2 oz. (45 g) margarine

   3 1/3 oz. (95 g) .... each: cake flour
   beaten eggs

1. Preheat oven to 180°C (355°F). Cream **1** until light and fluffy (illus 1). Add evaporated milk and beaten eggs, then add milk powder until well blended. Divide the filling into 16 portions.
2. Divide the dough into 16 equal portions, shape each dough into ball (illus 2). Cover with damp cloth and let rest for 10 minutes.
3. Flatten each piece of dough and wrap a portion of filling inside. Press to seal and place the sealed side underneath. Place the rolls on a greased baking sheet 4-5cm (1 1/2" - 2 ") apart. Cover with a damp cloth and let rise in a warm, damp place until doubled (about 90 minutes).
4. Cream **2** until light and fluffy, add beaten eggs and beat until smooth. Beat in cake flour and blend well. Place the batter into a piping bag.
5. Pipe the batter spirally onto the rolls (illus 3). Bake until golden (about 15-18 minutes). Remove from the oven and knock the baking sheet against a table for easy removal of the rolls.

咖哩麵包 · Curry Buns

軟式甜麵糊	1份
絞肉	375公克
沙拉油	1大匙
水	1/2杯
洋蔥	400公克
咖哩粉	1 1/2大匙
麵包粉	1 1/2杯
1 低筋麵粉	1 1/2大匙
鹽	1 1/2小匙
細砂糖	1小匙
味精	少許

1. 烤箱預熱至180℃備用。
2. 洋蔥洗淨切碎；鍋熱入油1大匙燒熱，入洋蔥炒至透明狀（圖1）後，隨入咖哩粉拌炒均勻，再入絞肉炒勻，續入 **1** 料及水拌炒至濃稠狀時即為咖哩餡，盛起待涼，分成16等份。
3. 麵糊分成16等份，用手搓圓，蓋上扭乾的濕布醒10分鐘，再擀成直徑12公分之圓片，包入1份咖哩餡，捏成餃子狀後（圖2），每個麵糰均勻沾水，再沾麵包粉（圖3），接縫處朝下置於烤盤上，麵糰間隔4至5公分，再蓋上扭乾之濕布，放在溫暖潮濕的地方發酵至2倍大（約90分鐘）。
4. 將麵糰入烤箱烤至上色（約14－15分鐘），取出時連同烤盤輕摔一下即可。

1	quantity basic sweet roll dough
14 oz. (400 g)	onion
13 1/4 oz. (375 g)	ground pork
1 1/2 T.	curry powder
1 T.	salad oil
1 1/2 C.	bread crumbs
1/2 C.	water
1 1 1/2 T.	cake flour
1 1/2 t.	salt
1/2 t.	granulated sugar

1. Preheat oven to 180°C (355°F).
2. Wash and chop the onions. Heat a wok and add 1 T oil. Stir fry the onions until transparent (illus 1), add in curry powder and mix well. Add the pork and stir fry. Add **1** and water; stir fry until thickened. This is the curry filling. Remove and leave to cool. Divide the filling into 16 portions.
3. Divide the dough into 16 equal portions. Roll each piece into a ball and cover with a damp cloth for 10 minutes. Roll the balls with a rolling pin into 12 cm (5") round pieces. Wrap a portion of filling inside a dough piece and pinch into a crescent ravioli (illus. 2). Sprinkle on water evenly and dip into bread crumbs (illus. 3). Place them on a baking sheet 4 - 5 cm (1 1/2" - 2 ") apart. Cover with a damp cloth. Let rise in a warm, damp place until doubled (about 90 minutes).
4. Bake until golden (about 14 - 15 minutes). Remove from oven and knock the baking sheet against a table for easy removal of the buns.

洋蔥培根麵包 · Onion-Bacon Knots

高筋麵粉	350 公克
洋蔥	250 公克
培根	165 公克
奶油	40 公克
1 高筋麵粉	150 公克
鹽	5 公克
2 水	175 公克
細砂糖	15 公克
乾酵母	5 公克
蛋	1 個
3 細砂糖	85 公克
水	80 公克
奶粉	10 公克
乾酵母	5 公克

1. 烤箱預熱至１８０℃；培根及洋蔥切碎；準備一不沾鍋備用。
2. 鍋熱入培根以小火炒至出油後，入洋蔥拌炒至呈透明狀後（7至8分鐘），盛起置於餐巾紙上將多餘的湯汁吸乾，待涼備用。
3. 麵糰做法請先參照「軟式甜麵糰」作法1至2步驟。
4. 洋蔥培根分2至3次揉入麵糰中（圖１）；將麵糰拿起，往下摔打，對折後，換邊握住再摔打一下，以此方法連續摔打至麵糰光滑後（約２００次），蓋上扭乾之濕布鬆弛１０分鐘。
5. 麵糰分成１６等份，用手搓圓，蓋上扭乾之濕布鬆弛１０分鐘。
6. 每個小麵糰搓成２０-２５公分之均勻棒狀（圖２），再打個活結（圖３），置於塗有奶油之烤盤上，麵糰間隔4至5公分，蓋上扭乾之濕布，放在溫暖潮濕的地方發酵至2倍大（約９０分鐘）。
7. 將麵糰入烤箱烤至上色（約１４至１５分鐘），取出時連同烤盤輕摔一下，麵包表面再趁熱塗上奶油即可。

12⅓ oz. (350g)	bread flour
9 oz.(250 g)	onion
6 oz.(165 g)	bacon
1½ oz.(40 g)	butter or margarine
1 5⅓ oz.(150 g)	bread flour
1 t.	salt
2 ¾ C.	water
½ oz.(15 g)	granulated sugar
1 t.	active dry yeast
1	egg
3 3 oz. (85 g)	granulated sugar
⅓ C.	water
⅓ oz.(10 g)	milk powder
1 t.	active dry yeast

1. Preheat oven to 180°C (355°F). Chop bacon and onion.
2. Heat a Teflon-coated frying pan, fry chopped bacon. Add chopped onion and fry until transparent (about 7 - 8 minutes). Remove onto a kitchen towel-covered plate to drain off the fat. Leave to cool.
3. Prepare the dough as Basic Sweet Roll (page 65), step 1 to step 2.
4. Divide onion-bacon mixture to 3 portions, knead the mixture into the dough; Qouter skin dough: one portion at a time (illus. 1). Throw the dough against the working table, fold it into half. Then hold the dough on one side and throw once again on the other side of the dough. Repeat the process until the dough is smooth (about 200 times). Cover with damp cloth and let rest for 10 minutes.
5. Divide the dough into 16 equal portions. Shape each dough into a ball. Cover with damp cloth and let rest for 10 minutes.
6. Roll each ball into 20 - 25 cm long strips (illus. 2), then tie a loose knot (illus. 3). Place them on a greased baking sheet, keep 4 - 5 cm (1½" - 2") apart. Cover with damp cloth and let rise in a warm, damp place until doubled (about 90 minutes).
7. Bake until golden (about 14 - 15 minutes). Remove from oven and knock the baking sheet lightly against the table for easy removal of the bread knots. Brush butter or margarine on the tops while still warm.

菠蘿麵包 · Rolls with Scaly Crust

軟式甜麵糰 1份
蛋黃液 .... 少許
高筋麵粉 .... 少許

菠蘿皮：
低筋麵粉 150公克
糖粉 65公克
蛋 30公克

1｜白油 50公克
　　酥油 30公克
　　奶油 10公克

1. 烤箱預熱至１８０℃；麵糰分成１６等份，用手搓圓，蓋上扭乾之濕布鬆弛１０分鐘。
2. **1** 料攪拌均勻後，入糖粉拌勻，再入蛋拌勻，最後入低筋麵粉，用拌壓的方式使之均勻（不可壓太久或次數太多，以免出油），分成１６等份即為菠蘿皮。
3. 用噴水器在麵糰上噴一層水（不可用手沾水噴灑，以免水氣太多，麵糰太濕），取一麵糰沾上一份菠蘿皮，菠蘿皮上沾少許高筋麵粉（圖１），再以右手指推壓麵糰（圖２），使菠蘿皮均勻擴散並包住 ²/₃ 麵糰（圖３）。
4. 將菠蘿皮朝上，置於塗有奶油之烤盤上，然後將每個麵糰刷上蛋黃液，放在溫暖潮濕的地方發酵至２倍大（約９０分鐘）。
5. 將麵糰入烤箱中層烤１０至１５分鐘，待麵包底部上色，麵包表面顏色不會太深時，取出，連同烤盤輕摔一下即可。

---

1 .... quantity basic sweet roll dough

Scaly crust:
5 1/3 oz. (150 g) .. cake flour
2 1/3 oz. (65 g) .... powdered sugar
1 oz. (30 g) .... eggs

as needed: bread flour, beaten egg yolks

1｜1 2/3 oz. (50 g) .... shortening
　　1 oz. (30 g) .. butter oil substitue
　　1/3 oz. (10 g) .. butter or margarine

1. Preheat oven to 180°C (355°F). Divide the dough into 16 equal portions. Shape each dough into a ball and cover with damp cloth to rest for 10 minutes.
2. Beat **1** until well blended, then add powdered sugar and eggs. Mix in cake flour, press down on the dough to barely mixed (do not knead or press too much to prevent the fat oozing out). Divide the crust dough into 16 equal portions.
3. Spray a thin layer of water over the sweet roll dough balls (do not over-wet the dough, only a thin layer of mist). Place a portion of crust dough on a portion of roll dough. Dust each crust dough with a dash of bread flour (illus. 1). Press out the crust dough with your thumb (illus. 2) to cover two thirds of the sweet roll dough (illus. 3).
4. Place the rolls on a greased baking sheet, crust side up. Brush on a thin layer of beaten egg yolks. Let rise in a warm, damp place until doubled (about 90 minutes).
5. Bake for 10 - 15 minutes, or until the bottom of the rolls turn golden and the tops light golden. Remove from the oven and knock the baking sheet against a table for easy removal of the rolls.

全麥麵包 · Whole Wheat Bread

高筋麵粉	250公克
全麥麵粉	250公克
奶油	40公克
鹽	5公克

1
- 水 240公克
- 糖 60公克
- 奶粉 10公克
- 酵母 5公克
- 蛋 1個

1. 烤箱預熱至１８０℃；高筋麵粉、全麥麵粉、鹽混和一起後，入拌勻之 **1** 料內搓揉至光滑，再將奶油揉入麵糰內。
2. 將麵糰拿起，往下摔打，對折後，換邊握住再摔打一下，以此方法連續摔打至麵糰光滑後（約２００次），蓋上扭乾之濕布醱酵９０分鐘。
3. 麵糰分成４等份，用手搓圓（圖１），蓋上扭乾之濕布鬆弛１０分鐘；桌面及擀麵棍上撒上高筋麵粉，把每份麵糰擀成橢圓形，再密實的捲起（圖２），接縫處捏緊朝下，置於塗有奶油之烤盤上，蓋上扭乾之濕布，放在溫暖潮濕的地方發酵至２倍大（約９０分鐘）。
4. 在每個麵糰上用沾有麵粉的刀子劃３斜刀後（圖３），入烤箱烤至上色（約２０至２５分鐘），取出時連同烤盤輕摔一下，麵包表面再趁熱塗上奶油即可。

9 oz. (250 g) bread flour
8⁴/₅ oz. (250 g) whole wheat flour
1¹/₂ oz. (40 g) ...... butter or margarine
1 t. .... salt

1
- 1 C. .... water
- 2 oz. (60 g) .... sugar
- ¹/₃ oz. (10 g) .... milk powder
- 1 t. ...... active dry yeast
- 1 .... egg

1. Preheat oven to 180°C (355°F). Sift together bread flour, whole wheat flour, and salt. Mix with **1** and knead until smooth. Then knead in the butter or margarine.
2. Hold the dough and throw it against a table; fold into halves and throw once on the other side. Repeat until the dough smooth and shinny (about 200 times. Cover with damp cloth and let raise for 90 minutes.
3. Divide the dough into 4 portions. Shape each piece of dough into a ball (illus. 1). Cover with damp cloth and let rest for 10 minutes. Dust the working table and rolling pin with flour. Roll each dough into oblong shape, tightly roll it up with the side underneath (illus. 2). Place them on a greased baking sheet. Cover with damp cloth and leave in a warm, damp place to rise until doubled (about 90 minutes).
4. Score the tops with a flour knife (illus. 3), bake until golden (about 20 - 25 minutes). Remove from oven and knock the baking sheet against the table for easy removal of the bread. Brush the tops with butter or margarine while still warm.

圓頂奶油吐司 · Domed Top Tin Loaf

高筋麵粉 ... 1000 公克(100%)
奶油 .... 160 公克(16%)
鹽 .... 10 公克(1%)

1
水 .... 460 公克(46%)
細砂糖 .... 160 公克(16%)
蛋（淨重）160 公克(16%)
乾酵母 .... 10 公克(1%)

1. 烤箱預熱至１７０℃；高筋麵粉與鹽過篩至攪拌缸裡；奶油置室溫下軟化備用。
2. **1** 料拌勻，倒入攪拌缸內，用機器以慢速攪打至均勻即轉中速，打至麵糰光滑後，再入奶油用慢速攪打至奶油和入麵糰內，即可轉中速打至麵糰拉開呈薄膜狀（圖１），取出，放入塗油之鋼盆內，蓋上扭乾之濕布發酵９０分鐘。
3. 麵糰分成４等份，每份麵糰用手搓圓，置桌面上鬆弛１０分鐘，再用擀麵棍擀成橢圓形後，密實的捲起，置於塗油之烤盤上使之鬆弛（約１５至２０分鐘）。
4. 把每份麵糰擀成寬約１９公分之方形，再密實的捲起（圖２），接縫處朝下，分別置於塗油之20.5x10x11 cm模裡，蓋上扭乾之濕布，放在溫暖潮濕的地方發酵至模型的九分滿（約９０分鐘）。
5. 將麵糰入烤箱下層烤２５至３０分鐘，其間須將麵包調頭，以便均勻上色，並同時塗上奶油以增加麵包的香味（若麵包顏色已深而時間未到時，可蓋上一張白紙（圖３），以防麵包顏色繼續加深）。
6. 麵包烤好取出時，連同模型輕摔一下，趁熱將麵包扣出，並在表面塗上一層奶油即可。

$2^1/_5$ lb. (1000 g) bread flour (100%)
$5^1/_2$ oz. (160 g) .... butter or margarine (16%)
$1/_3$ oz. (10 g) .... salt (1%)
4 .... 450 g loaf tins

1
2 C. .... water (46%)
$5^1/_2$ oz. (160 g)............... granulated sugar (16%)
$5^1/_2$ oz. (160 g) eggs (net weight) (16%)
$1/_3$ oz. (10 g) .... active dry yeast (1%)

1. Preheat oven to 170°C (340°F). Sift bread flour and salt together into a large electric mixing bowl. Soften butter or margarine at room temperature.
2. Mix **1** in a large bowl. Beat at low speed until well blended, change to medium speed and mix until the dough is smooth. Cut in butter or margarine at low speed until well-mixed. Again change to medium speed and mix until the dough can be stretched into a thin sheet (illus. 1). Remove from the mixer and place in a greased bowl; cover with damp cloth and let rise for 90 minutes.
3. Divide the dough into 4 equal portions, knead into balls and let rest on the working table for 10 minutes. Roll each dough into a oblong piece with a rolling pin, then roll it tightly up into a cylinder. Place them on a greased baking sheet to rest for 15 to 20 minutes.
4. With a rolling pin, roll each dough into a 19 cm (9.5") square piece. Then roll tightly up with the end opening underneath (illus. 2). Place each piece of dough in greased tin loaf (8"x4"x4") and cover with damp cloth. Let them rise in a warm, damp place until the bulk has filled 90 % of the tin loaf (about 90 minutes).
5. Bake for 25 - 30 minutes. Turn the direction of the tins once during the baking to obtain even coloring of the tops. At the same time, brush with butter or margarine once. (Cover with paper if the top browns too soon) (illus. 3).
6. Remove from the oven. Knock the tins against a table for easy removal of the bread. Turn out the bread and brush the tops with butter or margarine while still warm.

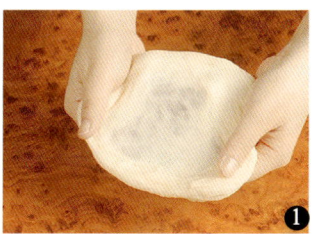  

圓頂葡萄乾吐司 · Raisin Tin Loaf

高筋麵粉	1000公克
葡萄乾	250公克
白油	100公克
鹽	15公克

1
- 蘭姆酒 1/4杯
- 熱開水 1杯

2
- 水 500公克
- 細砂糖、蛋 ... 各100公克
- 乾酵母 10公克

1. 烤箱預熱至１７０℃；葡萄乾泡入**1**料內至變軟（約１小時）撈起，瀝乾備用。
2. 高筋麵粉及鹽過篩至攪拌缸內；倒入拌勻的**2**料內，用機器以慢速攪拌均勻即轉中速，打至麵糊光滑，再入白油用慢速打至白油和入麵糊內，即轉中速打至麵糊拉開呈薄膜狀（圖１），再入葡萄乾用慢速攪至均勻後，放入塗油之鋼盆內，蓋上扭乾之濕布發酵９０分鐘。
3. 麵糊分成４等份，每份麵糊用手搓圓，置桌面上鬆弛１０分鐘，再用擀麵棍擀成橢圓形後，密實的捲起（圖２），置於塗油之烤盤上使之鬆弛約１５至２０分鐘。
4. 把每份麵糊擀成寬約１９公分之方形，再密實的捲起，接縫處朝下，分別置於塗油之20.5×10×11cm模裡，蓋上扭乾之濕布，放在溫暖潮濕的地方發酵至模型的九分滿（約９０分鐘）。
5. 將麵糊入烤箱底層烤１０分鐘後，表面蓋上一張白紙（圖３）續烤１５至２０分鐘，其間須將麵包調頭，以便均勻上色。
6. 麵包烤好取出時，連同模型輕摔一下，趁熱將麵包扣出，並在表面塗上一層奶油即可。

■ 烤箱溫度若有上下火、則將烤箱預熱至上火１００℃、下火２００℃烤２５至３０分鐘即可。

---

2 1/5 lb. (1000 g)	bread flour
9 oz. (250 g)	raisins
3 1/2 oz. (100 g)	shortening
1/2 oz. (15 g)	salt

1
- 1/4 C. .... rum
- 1 C. .... hot water

2
- 2 C. .... water
- 3 1/2 oz. (100 g) each: granulated sugar, egg
- 1/3 oz. (10 g) .... active dry yeast

1. Preheat oven to 170°C (340°F). Soak the raisins in **1** until soft (about 1 hour), remove and drain.
2. Sift flour and salt into a large electric mixer bowl. Pour in well-mixed **2**, beat first with low speed and then turn the speed to medium; beat until the dough is smooth. Add the shortening and beat with low speed until well blended, then turn the speed to medium and beat until the dough is cohesive (illus. 1). Fold in the raisins and mix well. Place the dough in a large greased bowl, cover with a damp cloth and allow the dough to rise in a warm place for 90 minutes.
3. Divide the dough into 4 equal parts, shape each piece of dough into balls and let them rest for 10 minutes. Roll them into oblong shapes and then tightly roll them up (illus. 2). Let them rest on a greased baking sheet for 15 to 20 minutes.
4. Roll each piece of dough into a 19 cm wide square, tightly roll it up. With the opening side down, place each piece of dough in a greased tin loaf. Cover with a wet cloth and allow it to rise in a warm place until the bulk fills 90% of the tin loaf (about 90 minutes).
5. Bake for 25 to 30 minutes. The loaf must be turned once during baking to even the outer coloring. (In the case of over browning of the top, cover with white paper) (illus. 3).
6. Remove from the oven. Knock the tin and turn out the bread while warm. Brush the loaves with butter.

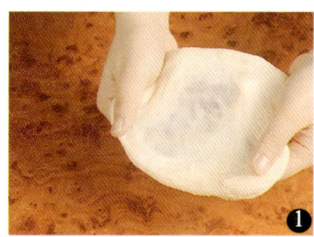

五峰山形白吐司 · Hilly Loaf

高筋麵粉	1000公克
鹽	20公克
白油	10公克
900公克吐司模	2個

①
- 水 620公克
- 細砂糖 50公克
- 奶粉 20公克
- 乾酵母 10公克

1. 烤箱預熱至170℃；麵糰攪拌過程請參照「圓頂奶油吐司」作法1至2。
2. 麵糰分成10等份，每份麵糰用手搓圓，置桌面上鬆弛10分鐘，每個麵糰用擀麵棍擀成橢圓形後，密實的捲起，置於塗油之烤盤上使之鬆弛（約15至20分鐘）。
3. 把麵糰擀成寬約9公分之長方形（圖1），再密實的捲起（圖2），接縫處朝下，一起置於塗油之32.5x11x11.5cm模裡，每個吐司模放5份麵糰（圖3），由兩旁平均放置，蓋上扭乾之濕布，放在溫暖潮濕的地方發酵至模型的九分滿（約90分鐘）。
4. 將麵糰入烤箱底層烤30至35分鐘，其間須將麵包調頭，以便均勻上色，（若麵包顏色已深而時間未到時，可蓋上一張白紙，以防麵包顏色繼續加深）。
5. 麵包烤好取出時，連同模型輕摔一下，趁熱將麵包扣出，並在表面塗上一層奶油即可。

2 ⅕ lb. (1000 g) bread flour
⅔ oz. (20 g) .... salt
⅓ oz. (10 g) .... shortening

①
- 2 ⅗ C. .... water
- 1 ⅔ oz. (50g) .... granulated sugar
- ⅔ oz. (20 g) .... milk powder
- ⅓ oz. (10 g) .... active dry yeast

1. Preheat oven to 170°C (340F°). Prepare the dough as Domed Top Tin Loaf, step 1 and step 2.
2. Divide the dough into 10 equal portions, knead into balls and let rest for 10 minutes. Roll each piece of dough into an oblong piece with a rolling pin, then roll it up tightly. Place on a greased baking sheet to rest for 15 to 20 minutes.
3. Roll each piece of dough into a 9 cm (3 ½") square (illus. 1), then roll it up tightly (illus. 2) with the end opening underneath. Place five pieces in a loaf tin (12"x4"x4") (illus. 3) and cover with damp cloth. Let rise in a warm, damp place until filling 90 % of the tin (about 90 minutes).
4. Bake for 30 to 35 minutes. Turn the direction of the tins once during baking to obtain even coloring on the top. (Cover with a piece of white paper if the top browns too soon).
5. Remove from the oven. Knock the tins against a table for easy removal of the bread. Invert out the bread and brush the surface with butter or margarine while still warm.

More Wei-Chuan Cook Books

純青出版社
劃撥帳號：12106299
地址：台北市松江路125號4樓
電話：(02)2508-4331、2506-3564
傳真：(02)2507-4902

Distributor: Wei-Chuan Publishing
1455 Monterey Pass Rd., #110
Monterey Park, CA 91754, U.S.A.
Tel: (323)2613880・2613878
Fax: (323)2613299

家常菜
- 226道菜
- 200頁
- 中文版

營養便當
- 147道菜
- 96頁
- 中文版

家常100
- 100道菜
- 96頁
- 中英對照

Favorite Chinese Dishes
- 100 recipes
- 96 pages
- Chinese/English Bilingual

素食
- 84道菜
- 120頁
- 中英對照

Vegetarian Cooking
- 84 recipes
- 120 pages
- Chinese/English Bilingual

健康素
- 76道菜
- 96頁
- 中英對照

Simply Vegetarian
- 76 recipes
- 96 pages
- Chinese/English Bilingual

微波食譜第一冊
- 62道菜
- 112頁
- 中英對照

Microwave Cooking Chinese Style
- 62 recipes
- 112 pages
- Chinese/English Bilingual

微波食譜第二冊
- 76道菜
- 128頁
- 中英對照

Microwave Cooking Chinese Style 2
- 76 recipes
- 128 pages
- Chinese/English Bilingual

養生家常菜
- 80道菜
- 96頁
- 中英對照

Chinese Home Cooking for Health
- 80 recipes
- 96 pages
- Chinese/English Bilingual

實用烘焙
- 77道點心
- 96頁
- 中英對照

International Baking Delight
- 77 recipes
- 96 pages
- Chinese/English Bilingual

飲茶食譜
- 88道菜
- 128頁
- 中英對照

Chinese Dim Sum
- 88 recipes
- 128 pages
- Chinese/English Bilingual

養生藥膳
- 73道菜
- 128頁
- 中英對照

Chinese Herb Cooking for Health
- 73 recipes
- 128 pages
- Chinese/English Bilingual

廣東菜
- 75道菜
- 96頁
- 中英對照

Chinese Cuisine Cantonese Style
- 75 recipes
- 96 pages
- Chinese/English Bilingual

嬰幼兒食譜
- 140道菜
- 104頁
- 中文版

無油煙食譜
- 46道菜
- 68頁/菊16開
- 中文版

快手菜食譜
- 49道菜
- 68頁/菊16開
- 中文版

美容餐食譜
- 50道菜
- 68頁/菊16開
- 中文版

下午茶食譜
- 40道菜
- 68頁/菊16開
- 中文版

米食-家常篇
- 84道菜
- 96頁
- 中英對照

米食-傳統篇
- 82道菜
- 96頁
- 中英對照

麵食-家常篇
- 91道菜
- 96頁
- 中英對照

麵食-精華篇
- 87道菜
- 96頁
- 中英對照

美味小菜
- 92道菜
- 96頁
- 中英對照

Rice Home Cooking
- 84 recipes
- 96 pages
- Chinese/English Bilingual

Rice Traditional Cooking
- 82 recipes
- 96 pages
- Chinese/English Bilingual

Noodles Home Cooking
- 91 recipes
- 96 pages
- Chinese/English Bilingual

Noodles Classical Cooking
- 87 recipes
- 96 pages
- Chinese/English Bilingual

Appetizers
- 92 recipes
- 96 pages
- Chinese/English Bilingual

四川菜
- 115道菜
- 96頁
- 中英對照

上海菜
- 91道菜
- 96頁
- 中英對照

台灣菜
- 73道菜
- 120頁
- 中英對照

庖廚偏方 庖廚錦囊 庖廚樂
- 中文版

Chinese Cuisine Szechwan Style
- 115 recipes
- 96 pages
- Chinese/English Bilingual

Chinese Cuisine Shanghai Style
- 91 recipes
- 96 pages
- Chinese/English Bilingual

Chinese Cuisine Taiwanese Style
- 73 recipes
- 120 pages
- Chinese/English Bilingual

味全家政班

味全家政班創立於民國五十年，經過三十餘年的努力，它不只是國內歷史最悠久的家政研習班，更成為一所正式學制之外的專門學校。

創立之初，味全家政班以教授中國菜及研習烹飪技術為主，因教學成果良好，備受各界讚譽，乃於民國五十二年，增闢插花、工藝、美容等各門專科，精湛的師資，教學內容的充實，深獲海內外的肯定與好評。

三十餘年來，先後來班參與研習的學員已近二十萬人次，學員的足跡遍及台灣以外，更有許多國外的團體或個人專程抵台，到味全家政班求教，在習得中國菜烹調的精髓後，或返回居住地經營餐飲業，或擔任家政教師，或獲聘為中國餐廳主廚者大有人在，成就倍受激賞。

近年來，味全家政班亟力研究開發改良中國菜餚，並深入國際間，採集各種精緻、道地美食，除了樹立中華文化「食的精神」外，並將各國烹飪口味去蕪存菁，擷取地方特色。為了確保這些研究工作更加落實，我們特將這些集合海內外餐飲界與研發單位的精典之作，以縝密的拍攝技巧與專業編輯，出版各式食譜，以做傳承。

薪傳與發揚中國烹飪的藝術，是味全家政班一貫的理念，日後，也將秉持宗旨，永續不輟。

Wei-Chuan Cooking School

Since its establishment in 1961, Wei-Chuan Cooking School has made a continuous commitment toward improving and modernizing the culinary art of cooking and special skills training. As a result, it is the oldest and most successful school of its kind in Taiwan.

In the beginning, Wei-Chuan Cooking School was primarily teaching and researching Chinese cooking techniques. However, due to popular demand, the curriculum was expanded to cover courses in flower arrangements, handcrafts, beauty care, dress making and many other specialized fields by 1963.

The fact that almost 200,000 students, from Taiwan and other countries all over the world, have matriculated in this school can be directly attributed to the high quality of the teaching staff and the excellent curriculum provided to the student's. Many of the graduates have become successful restaurant owners and chefs, and in numerous cases, respected teachers.

While Wei-Chuan Cooking School has always been committed to developing and improving Chinese cuisine, we have recently extended our efforts toward gathering information and researching recipes from different provinces of China. With the same dedication to accuracy and perfection as always, we have begun to publish these authentic regional gourmet recipes for our devoted readers. These new publications will continue to reflect the fine tradition of quality our public has grown to appreciate and expect.